Regency England Undressed
Harriette Wilson, the Greatest Courtesan of her Age

Harriette Wilson

Regency England Undressed

Harriette Wilson, the Greatest
Courtesan of her Age

Lesley Blanch

BookBlast ePublishing
LONDON

First published in New York in 1955 by Gryphon Books, and in London in 1957 by John Murray, as the Introduction to *The Game of Hearts: Harriette Wilson's Memoirs. Interspersed with excerpts from the Confessions of Julia Johnstone, her rival.*

This electronic and print-on-demand edition published in 2016 by BookBlast ePublishing, a division of BookBlast Limited, P.O. Box 20184, London W10 5AU.

Mobi ISBN 978-0-9933552-0-2
Epub ISBN 978-0-9933552-1-9
Print ISBN 978-0-9933552-2-6

BookBlast has been online since 2000 and is trademarked in the UK and the US. Visit www.bookblast.com to find out more about the authors and their books. Scanned by BookBlast Ltd, London.

Conversion by Mousemat Design Limited, Kent BR6 8HR.
Illustrated with engravings from the period.
Cover illustrations by Lesley Blanch. www.lesleyblanch.com

ANNE SEBBA, THE SPECTATOR:

What do a modern New York psychoanalyst and a Regency London courtesan have in common? Both offer escape, relaxation and individual attention; both are expensive. "In place of the alcove there is the analyst's office. But basically the functions of both analyst and courtesan have the same principle," explains Lesley Blanch in her expansive introduction to the memoirs of the most famous of English courtesans, Harriette Wilson.

1

Harriette Wilson viewing Lord Craven
while saling at Brighton

THE NINETEENTH CENTURY was an age of great personalities, a last splendid flowering before twentieth-century anonymity and mass living engulfed them in its drab tide. England was always a stronghold of eccentrics and individualists. At this moment they had reached their apogee. But beside the Wellingtons, Beckfords, Byrons or Lady Hester Stanhopes of the age, a small, giddy shade is still remembered with delight, if not with honour. Harriette Wilson's life was deplorable — but how readable! She emerges from her *Memoirs* and other contemporary sources as a most engaging creature — though that is, after all, what would be expected of the most celebrated courtesan of her day (and one, moreover, who really relished her calling). There is always an especial interest in memoirs and journals which give us an unselfconscious, eyewitness account of the daily life of other ages; the vivid picture of everyday, medieval family life that emerges from the Paston letters could not be made so real to us by any other medium. The court of Louis XIV, with all its majesty and brittle intrigue, is brought to life for us by the pen of St. Simon. Pepys's odd jumble of household accounts, Stuart excesses, foreign policies and his private pornographic jottings make Restoration England relive for us. Perhaps an added zest attaches to those memoirs which verge on the *chroniques scandaleuses*, especially where they concern the private life of the great. Casanova's memoirs cannot be called everyday life, but they are certainly good reading — a raree show of eighteenth-century European gallantry in the raw. The value of the great diarists often lies less in their personality than in their background. Creevey, sly wag, Greville, Gronow, Thomas Raikes, Mrs. Arbuthnot — all of them have created for us scenes which we remember principally because of their background: Regency London.

But Harriette Wilson's *Memoirs* stand apart. By nature of her profession a courtesan's memoirs must deal primarily with herself and give a close-range portrait of the men she came to know. Harriette's own evocation of the Regency scene is not so much a panorama as an interior it serves to sharpen our interest.

It might be asked why the memoirs of a courtesan, deliberately written with an eye to blackmail, should be of particular interest to us; but even if Harriette did extort money for suppressing, or removing, some of her memories of the great and the rich, it does not lessen the intensely personal authenticity of the pictures she paints. She is mischievous rather than malicious, outrageous but not pornographic. As Sir Walter Scott wrote: 'H.W. beats [the memoirs of] Con Philips and Anne Bellamy and all former demi-reps out and out.' She gives us a microcosm of one particular stratum of London life where she ruled supreme. She is her own Boswell. How could such a chronicle fail to enthrall?

Then, too, by the time we have followed Harriette through so many vicissitudes we have grown to love her — however monstrous her behaviour. We see why Harriette — shabbily treated by the Duke of Beaufort, done out of her pension, her looks and youth gone, falling from fashion, penniless, victim of her own extravagances, fighting to keep a hold on Rochfort, her fancy man — began to cast about desperately for a means of raising money. What else had she to sell now but her memories? Thus, fighting for life, she wrote the *Memoirs* — for money, not out of a clinging nostalgia nor, as has been said, for spite. At what stage of her work she thought of offering certain victims the chance of buying themselves out we do not know, nor do we know whether this was her own idea or that of Stockdale, her enterprising publisher, or the malign influence of Rochfort. Nor do we know how many men bought themselves out. Harriette kept her word; those who paid escaped and, after all, the price she asked was not exorbitant, especially since the men she approached were all wealthy and privileged. ('She attacks no poor man, no single man, they cannot pay, or do not fear her calumnies.') Still, by the time she struck, just as she had fallen, so they had, in the main, risen to positions of dignity and eminence and could ill afford to appear in such a context. Consequently many of them paid up, and the reader is the poorer.

Harriette Wilson lived among and was an integral part of a wealthy society where privilege, arrogance and leisure flourished. This is the courtesan's natural background; once these things disappear, particularly the wealth which leisure implies, the courtesan is doomed. She does not flourish in an industrial age. She may be said to have vanished with the nineteenth century, the first half of which, specifically, was the heyday of all those women whose personality and style, more than beauty alone, were such that they could command, besides large sums of money, independence and respect. The basic difference between the courtesan and the prostitute was not so much a question of class as of personality. The legendary courtesans provided more than sex alone. In England, Harriette Wilson was an outstanding example of her profession. She was followed, in France, by Marie Duplessis. Between them these two widely different women personified their respective country and period, and between them they brought to a close the first half of the century and with it the great age of the classic and romantic courtesan.

True, there was a brilliant and superficially more striking era near the end of the century when the *grandes cocottes* such as Liane de Pougy, and Emillienne d'Alençon succeeded the Cora Pearls and Anna Deshons of the 1860s and 1870s. But it was a St. Martin's summer, a last blaze where extravagance and flamboyance were the keynote, a calculated extravagance, however, which was already tainted by big business methods.

Publicity was the new god of the industrial age and it changed the *demi-monde* too. These fabulous cocottes, or '*créatures*,' as they were called in the Paris salons, were, first of all, showpieces. Carriages, toilettes, jewels, even their whims, were calculated for effect; advertising had arrived, together with big business. An outward life of show came to occupy as important a place in the game as any alcove. The foyer, the 'other woman's establishment,' was suddenly less desirable than the best table at Maxim's, or a yacht. Suddenly, travel became fashionable; the great migratory trek from casino to spa, from winter resort to summer watering place had begun: Deauville, Biarritz, Monte Carlo, Biskra, Vichy.

The pace was as killing as the price, so that the actress, Mrs. Patrick Campbell, spoke for many men when she pronounced on "the deep peace of the double bed after the hurly-burly of the chaise-longue." The twentieth century cast a long shadow before it, ominous and forbidding, and *la vie galante*, high gallantry, and the courtesan were all doomed.

Today we see that economic pressure and mass living have been far more destructive to *la vie galante* than any morality drives. In fact, they have been the first and only force to oppose sexual freedom in the sense of which I speak, in the sense of destroying the courtesan and her world. Mass living implies mass thought. A society of leisure could afford to live individually, could afford to keep life in separate compartments. Men had homes, families, wives, mistresses, clubs, and two social lives, one shared with their wife, the other one independent of her. Today, everything is reduced to the minimum — call girl, massage parlour, or back seat.

Then it must be remembered that the decline of the marriage of convenience is also, in part, responsible for the decline of the courtesan. When such marriages were customary the husband generally went in search of other women and, when circumstances permitted, another foyer, or hearth. (Although today the distractions of sex can be obtained by varying degrees of expenditure, the maintenance of a separate establishment denotes a very high standard of living and leisure. It is, in fact, a luxury to which few men can now subscribe.)

In European polite society in the late eighteenth and early nineteenth centuries the wife, too, was conceded great freedom. The attentions of both *cicisbeo* and *cavaliere servente* were ambiguous. A man expected his first-born to be his own — but once the inheritance was firmly established with two or more little pledges, the wife was generally able to seek her diversions elsewhere, as her husband had done from the first. "One exists with one's husband — one lives with one's lover," says the Marquise de Vandenesse in Balzac's *Une fille d'Eve*.

In such a society, then, the courtesan played a very important part. She was not 'received,' but she had her own world — that hieratic *demi-monde* with its own etiquette and protocol. She never seems to have revolted against her exclusions or limitations. Perhaps she knew how firmly her half-world was entrenched behind the larger *beau monde* from which she drew her protectors. The courtesan derived from a society which surrounded sex not only with all those graces women once commanded, but also with that style men could once afford to demand.

She was, in fact, a *dame de compagnie* in the largest sense.

The courtesan was expected to provide all the shades of companionship without the oppressive limitations and implications of marriage. She offered not only the bed but the sofa, the alcove and the hearth, the dinner table and the salon — all save the nursery and the kitchen. Her conversation as well as her company was courted. Her personality as much as her person had a price. To be seen with her during a drive in the park, at a restaurant or in her box at the theatre was regarded as an achievement. In Harriette Wilson's day the young noblemen used to drive down from Oxford or Cambridge for the express purpose of obtaining an introduction to her as she held court in her opera box. This box was not only the courtesan's showcase, or shop window, but, according to her degree of fame, the gauge of her current lover's wealth and taste. Thus we see a system designed to surround the basic traffic with elegance.

In a society of individualists such as that of Regency England, Harriette Wilson had to match her own personality against those of the distinguished men who were her world. She was no beauty, but she was herself, like no one else, and her immense vitality, her wit and lively interest in terms, brought her to the top of her profession and made her the fashion. A merely lovely, compliant creature could not have stayed the course for long; she would have been just one more of the ranks of prostitutes who at that time, we are told, swarmed about the city of London.

And here we might speculate on how much education — not perhaps in the academic sense, but in that of general culture — Harriette acquired from her lovers, from years of association with men who, however much they might choose to masquerade as being interested only in the turf, prize-fighting and cards did, in fact, stem from a cultivated aristocracy. There are many ways of learning. Harriette, who left home at fifteen and spent more time in bed than most, spoke fluent French and seems to have been well-read. Her memoirs show her to have been far more than an agreeable rattle-pate. She was born witty; but I think she acquired a considerable culture, the art of conversation and letter writing, and a philosophic way of thought which she did

13

not owe to her family background, but rather to those men who were her protectors — men who, one might say, came to sleep but stayed to dine; men who, probably unconsciously, paid for their entertainment with more than a mere fee. After all they were among the best minds, the greatest wits of the age. She was on good terms with such men as Tom Sheridan, son of the playwright, Lord Alvanley, the famous wit, Luttrell, who was considered the most brilliant conversationalist of his day, Henry Brougham, the great advocate, the Duke of Wellington, and many more. Association with men of this calibre must have been an education in itself.

The finer shades of what might be described as pleasing are many. The prostitute, the courtesan, the *femme entretenue*, or kept woman, are all variations on the theme. Harriette Wilson falls into the category of courtesan chiefly because of her independent attitude, her selective approach. She changed her lovers as easily as her shoes, says Julia Johnstone, her rival. But while the prostitute is to be bought by anyone, the courtesan selects her patrons, and the *femme entretenue* is kept, in exclusivity, by one protector, to be entirely at his disposal. Although Harriette was, we imagine, kept in exclusivity, for certain stretches of time, by the Duke of Argyll, Lords Ponsonby and Worcester, and others besides, she was essentially a courtesan. Her exclusivity was relative; and except in the case of Lord Ponsonby, the love of her life, it is doubtful that she ever intended or wished to be the property of any one man. She liked variety, and had, on her own admission, *le diable au corps* — brisk appetites, wrote Balzac in 1838. 'See how perfectly the Dubarry fits the eighteenth century and Ninon de Lenclos the seventeenth century. These women are the poetry of their age. Laïs and Rhodope *are* Greece and Egypt.'

The flavour and tempo of an age is reflected in many ways:

in the curve of a corset, a taste in wines, the *argot* of the moment. Such trivialities conjure an epoch as sharply as historic headlines. The various glittering facets of *la vie galante*, too, are sharply evocative. Through the long mirrors that lined Josephine de Beauharnais' rooms in the rue Chantereine, we see not only the febrile post-revolutionary society, but Bonaparte as a lovesick First Consul. Intrigues behind the Franco-Prussian war were played out against the ormolu and plush salons of La Païva's establishment. Dumas and Gautier and Liszt and all Romantic Paris crowd into Marie Duplessis's box at the Funambules. Munich overboils into revolution on the steps of Lola Montez' house. Wellington returns from the Peninsular Campaign to court Harriette Wilson and, since her affections are otherwise engaged, she locks him out in a downpour.

Each nation, like each age, has its different idiom. The Greek hetaerae were votaries, a sect of beautiful and cultivated women, set apart, designed to please, to charm, as others were to breed. Greek logic saw things clearly: there were no half shades, no straggling ranks of amateurs, either way, whether to dull their delights, or threaten their domestic peace. The hetaerae were not only desirable as women, (though one of the most celebrated was positively plain), but they were schooled to provide the highest intellectual companionship too. (The Latin word *hetaera* derives from the Greek *hetaira* — a companion.) They consorted with the greatest statesmen and intellectuals, and were never admitted to the ranks until they had considerable attainments.

Turning eastward, where education has always sought to develop rather than extinguish the senses, as Gèrard de Nerval remarks wistfully, we find the same approach, the same blend of intellect and *volupté* combined in the traditions of Chinese gallantry. In Japan there was the stylized formality, as rigid and brilliant as the costumes, where the institution of the Yoshiwara Yuwaku, or professional prostitution, (both male and female), was the essence of Oriental formality, as are those accounts of tenth-century love affairs recounted by the Lady Murasaki in her *Tale of Genji*.

In Japan, too, there is that temple dedicated to some benign deity who favours prostitutes. The women make ceremonial pilgrimages to donate an animal figure; the temple swarms with these rather grotesque and Disney-like creatures, in every kind of substance. There are little whiskered snouts in gold, or jade, or coral, with ruby eyes or enamelled ears; giant beasts in bronze, life-sized ones in crystal, infinitesimally small ones in ivory or ebony. Their size and splendour vary according to the value of the affair for which the prostitute renders thanks.

Another, rather less formalized East is reflected in the person of Scheherazade, the storyteller of Bagdad, the slave girl whose conversational prowess, it is evident, outshone all the rest of her charms. Here we see a world of abandon and cunning, of cruel and capricious caliphs, a world where, to survive, a woman had to be more than merely beautiful.

A curiously muted, almost stealthy voluptuousness breathes from Carpaccio's paintings of Venetian prostitutes. Renaissance beauties sunning themselves on flat rooftops overlooking the Grand Canal. They braid one another's bleached golden hair, sit in attitudes of melancholy and repose, brooding over their pet doves, or perhaps their fading youth. They droop; they are clinging vines, as minor in key as the green ghostly waterways of Venice. For all that, they wielded considerable influence, socially and politically. They were considered as one of the city's ornaments, almost a matter of civic pride. People came from afar merely to witness the state appearances of these beauties of whom the Republic was so proud.

All the roaring bawdry of Shakespeare's Bankside life is embodied in Doll Tearsheet the strumpet, a match for anyone. All the gusto of Restoration England is in Moll Flanders, Daniel Defoe's whore. Captain Macheath's doxies step straight from a canvas by Hogarth, and early Georgian London lives around them, as it did when John Gay wrote *The Beggar's Opera*. Such women epitomize the more ephemeral aspects of pleasing; they could be had for a night or an hour. And to go forward in time, when Emma Crouch leaped from obscurity in London to become Cora Pearl, the most notorious of all the Parisian *demi-mondaines*, she always remained the trollop, the coarse, rampageous tart, regardless of her princely lovers and satin-hung boudoirs. However seductive, she was not a courtesan, (as was Marie Duplessis or Harriette Wilson), but rather '*la putain anglaise*,' whose conduct outraged even the men and women of her immediate circle, which is saying a great deal.

In the Marquise de Pompadour we find the perfect expression of both her nation and age. She too is the crystaliza-tion of a whole way of life, a whole school of taste, loosely described as *dix-huitième*. She is the apotheosis of the kept woman, a being set apart, mistress of the king, his inseparable companion. She was a woman of intellect, charm and wit, who held her lover in spite of, rather than because of, her flesh. It is well that she failed to respond to his ardour. It tired her; it bored her. But she remained supreme to the end simply by supplying those graces and distractions, that *companionship* which the monarch never found elsewhere. She wielded enormous influence; her subtle sway changed policies, launched fashions and established painters and poets. Her frown spelled failure; her smile, fortune. She intellectualized the passions, interpreting them with the same frivolous air of elegance and artificiality we see in the painting of Boucher, or Fragonard. She kept everything, even love, regulated by that excellent French sense of order and proportion which reached its highest expression in the writings of Voltaire, or the architecture of Versailles. She is often accused of having supplied the king with young girls at a little hunting box, the Pare aux Cerfs. Probably she did, rather in the manner of an intelligent *maîtresse de maison* employing extra help for the heavy work. It was a sensible solution, in an age at once practical and profligate, but never romantic.

Barely a century later, however, the Romantic heyday was to impose other standards. In the 1830s courtesans, and prostitutes too, were surrounded by a peculiarly emotional climate — especially those who fell by the way, who died young, of love, of consumption, of no matter what, so long as a pale cheek could shed a glistening tear, so long as renunciations and frustrations ensured a tragic ending to every love story. The archetype of all these romanticized daughters of joy is Marie Duplessis, the model for Dumas' Marguerite Gautier, and Verdi's Violetta, *La Traviata,* and who was in real life Alphonsine Plessis. When Dumas *fils* wrote the preface to the novel in which he immortalized her as *La Dame aux Camélias,* he spoke of her as ephemeral, the embodiment of a brief moment of emotion. '*La Dame aux Camélias* was written fifteen years ago; it could not be written today. Not only would it not be true — but it would not even be possible. One searches vainly for a woman who could inspire such emotion, who could develop such a love; who could make such a repentance, and such a sacrifice credible.' She was barely twenty-three when she died, but she had become a legend. Dickens; in Paris at the time, went to the auction of her possessions, and remarked that, to see the sorrow her loss occasioned, one might have believed it concerned a national hero, a Joan of Arc. Public enthusiasm knew no bounds when Eugène Sue bid for her prayer book. And Liszt, with all

Europe at his feet, and the ladies of every capital palpitating if he so much as glanced in their direction, found her 'the most perfect incarnation of Woman that has ever existed.' "A child, fallen asleep in a courtesan's bed," said her contemporaries, in ecstasies of grief. "A virgin that chance made a courtesan; a courtesan that could, by chance, as well be the purest virgin."

This worship of the courtesan is one of the most striking aspects of a general exaltation of love, physical, mystical and abstract, which reigned among the poets, painters and aristocracy during the period. When love was thus exalted as the greatest emotion man could experience, it follows that the courtesan, who was its high priestess, appeared as a sort of divinity. They saw in her the incarnation of all they desired — not only a woman, but an ideal; not only their mistress, but their Muse. They approached her with rapture and reverence, as an almost sacred being dedicated to the fulfillment of passion. No true Romantic, poet or dandy, could remain insensitive to one who could dispense the emotions which were their life's blood. The plain fact that she was paid, that her dispensations were to be bought, was seldom mentioned, or else it was glossed over in a tangle of high-flown phrases.

It was the flowering of an idealistic approach to free love — to love above all. "She has completed her life" was the fashionable way of saying that a woman had taken a lover; and though this phrase was applied not to the courtesan, but to the married woman, whether of the aristocracy or bourgeoisie, the same tone of complacency surrounded anything concerning the passions. Within the various economic limitations, each stratum of society had its own version of the amorous theme. Even the penniless poets and students of Murger's *Scenes de la Vie de Bohème* had their *lorettes*, or *grisettes*, those little working-girls who scraped their *sous* together to provide inspiration in the shape of a bottle of wine, offered along with their love. And the despised bourgeoisie, too, were united with the artists and the aristocracy in their craving for emotion — love for love's sake. The actress Marie Dorval spoke for her age when she wrote, 'Is it the senses which lure us on, eternally? No, it is a thirst for something more. It is the frenzy, the cravings to find true love which lures us and evades us, eternally.'

The dividing line between the *grande courtisane* and *grande amoureuse*, (or women who loved for love's sake alone), was often very slight. The history of Romantic Paris is a grand chain of emotional entanglements. *Ménage* overlapped *ménage*; men slept with one another's mistresses and wives; mothers and daughters were embroiled with the same lover; fathers supplanted their sons, who in turn poached on the paternal preserves; Victor Hugo snatches Alice Ozy from his son Charles, and Esther Guimont from his friend Emile de Girardin. In the name of love, this *monstre sacré*, this pseudo-mystical adulterer rides roughshod over so many, demands supreme sacrifices from his wife — from his mistress too, the lovely actress Juliette Drouet. Taking her, he imposes a bitter '*rédemption amoureuse*' of retirement, petty economies and domestic lectures, to which she submits voluptuously for years before she too is left to pine. How they carried on, those French Romantics! The ferment of passions was always kept at boiling-point.

When George Sand was unable to sweep Alfred de Musset out of his mother's sphere of influence, she found it quite normal to approach that lady and win her consent to the proposed Venetian idyll. Her eloquence was such that even maternal opposition ceded. Installed at Danieli's, the lovers were able to concentrate on further complications. Alfred soon contrived to inject a morbid note into their raptures. "You thought yourself my mistress, but you were my mother! We have committed incest!" (It was simpler in Regency England. It was 'Yes,' or 'No'; 'Tonight,' or 'Tomorrow night.') Presently, an unhappy termination to George and Alfred's love made everything seem well worthwhile. Besides, it provided both writers with a prodigious amount of copy. 'A Romantic's work is but an extension of his personality' wrote one romantic. George Sand and Alfred de Musset had lived every page of *Elle et Lui* and *La Confession d'un Enfant du Siècle*, their two versions of the liaison. In this spirit, it will be seen that unhappy endings, high tragedies of renunciation — or fulfillment — were not only *à la mode*, but good business too.

While both Regency London and Romantic Paris approached life hedonistically, and were preoccupied with the pleasures of the flesh, the Romantics spoke of body in terms of soul, especially a tormented one. Thus we see that both Harriette Wilson and Marie Duplessis were a perfect reflection of their moment, and were each an aspect of that Aspasian figure Balzac evoked. Both women shared, besides their calling, a certain generous simplicity which few of their rivals could claim. Neither was rapacious. Neither shared the insensate greed of Rachel, who, although the greatest actress of early nineteenth-century France, was never too romantic, too exalted, to keep a burning dark eye on the main chance. Her rapacity led her to sell her favours to the highest bidders; yet she knew how to put an over-bold admirer in his place. On receiving a note at the theatre during a performance, demanding her terms — '*ou, quand, combien?*' she sent back the following reply: '*Chez moi, ce soir, pour rien,*' a riposte which, while showing she could not resist the *bon mot* any more than the desire to rebuke a man arrogant enough to bid for her in such a way, was not, we feel, to be taken too literally.

Rachel never gave anything, least of all herself, for nothing.

The century which produced such women as Harriette and her rival demi-reps now seems as remote as any Neanderthal age. Yet there are still people alive who must recall a woman who might be described as her next-of-kin, Skittles, another very high-stepping charmer, her direct descendant, who may be said to have flourished till the day of her death.

Which leads me to reflect on that strange thread of chance, of fortune, which will lead two outwardly similar lives, one to success, the other to failure. Why should Harriette Wilson have sunk to oblivion and hard times, her youth and looks gone, and Skittles have lived to a ripe old age surrounded by an adoring circle of the most distinguished men? Skittles was perhaps the last of the spectacular English courtesans; she was born about 1840. She had, no doubt, more real beauty than Harriette, but beauty fades. Both were impudently gay, good company, and captivated not only the *coureurs* — men who, whether from psychological or physiological causes, chase after women indefatigably — but also men of an altogether different kidney. Harriette's personality alone seems to have won her the friendship of no less a figure than Henry Brougham, later the Lord Chancellor who, she says, (and it was never contradicted), gave her much valuable legal advice on how to proceed in her case against the Duke of Beaufort. Her professional successor, Skittles, entertained Mr. Gladstone to tea. Yet, both starting equal, both having the gift of acquiring friends, as well as lovers, for Skittles life ended well, for Harriette badly.

Skittles (Catherine Walters), too, had begun early, working in a skittie (or bowling) alley among the tough Lancashire crowds. Soon she was fair game for street rhymesters, hawking their scandal sheets from door to door:

In Liverpool, in days gone by,
For ha'pence and her wittles
A little girl by no means shy
Was settin' up the skittles.

Yet by the time she was established as a legend in London (having for some while been under the protection of the Duke of Devonshire) her personality was such that, in her pampered old age, being wheeled around the park where once she had driven her famous team of Orloff blacks, she was accompanied by the most distinguished statesmen and men of letters, who hung on her words. Her eyes were still enormous, violet, melting; she swore like a docker. She had enslaved so many different kinds of men — potmen, the Prince of Wales, the poet Wilfred Scawen Blunt. And to the end Lord Kitchener of Khartoum had been proud to push her bath-chair along the East Carriage Drive in Hyde Park.

By the middle of the nineteenth century, France, which usually set the tone in these matters, had replaced romantic miasmas with the harsh glitter of Second Empire gas lamps. Even Berlioz and Victor Hugo could no longer impose their impassioned vision on the hard base of French logic and materialism. Under the glare of the street lamps, we see, wafted in patchouli, the big-bosomed, tiny-booted street walkers of Constantin Guys' drawings. They mince along, inviting sidelong glances darting from below their frizzed bangs; they sprawl, sullen and lascivious, on curiously prim looking sofas while their patrons eye them arrogantly, like so much cattle. Nothing romantic here. Guys is the supreme painter of the *demi-monde*. No one knew better than he how to convey breeding in a horse, lack of it in a woman. It was Offenbach's world, the world of Cora Pearl, too, where the manners of the Empress Eugenie's court verged on those of the *demi-monde*. And, speaking of this age, we should perhaps recall Miss Howard, the English courtesan, whose love for the exiled Prince Louis Napoleon was proved in most positive terms. She placed her hard-won fortune at his disposal for the Bonapartist cause and was, not unnaturally, disappointed when, after becoming Emperor, Napoleon III married a Spanish commoner, Mademoiselle de Montijo.

In England, things were not following suit. Regency clarity was becoming shrouded in flannel. The snortings of the industrial age were accompanied by sniffs of disapproval. If Constantin Guys epitomized his era in France, Augustus Eggs' paintings of wayward, repentant matrons spoke for England. The rise of Victorian gentilities, and moral hypocrisy left no room for Harriette Wilson's tearing pace, her frank methods of livelihood, or any romantic miasmas. All were overcome by tidal waves of whitewash. The courtesans retreated to a colony of discreet villas around St. John's Wood, where high-walled gardens and roofed-in carriageways were effective in stilling any conjectures as to their visitors. 'Tarts' were never mentioned in polite society. The sons of those men whom Harriette Wilson had once enslaved busied themselves destroying all the papers or proof of their parents' infatuation. The *Memoirs* were burned, or languished out of reach on the top shelves of libraries.

There were still the 'flash cribs' around the Haymarket, which were frequented by the more draggled streetwalkers. And there were a bevy of 'pretty horse breakers' as they were called girls who could ride well, who worked with a livery stable, horse and girl being loosed on the Park along a ride then reserved exclusively for ladies of the profession, where both the rider and her mount were calculated to obtain an advantageous offer; and it was here that Miss Howard's paces were first admired.

But gradually the English came to look elsewhere, specifically to France, to the 'Gay Paree' of tourists' legend, for their pleasures. Edwardian society, which now embraced *parvenus* and a new aristocracy of wealth could afford the most scorching French *voluptés*, of which there were many levels: there were the rue Chabanais and the Bal Tabarin: there were the *grues*, those haggard and vicious creatures whom Toulouse-Lautrec loved to paint; but they had nothing to do with the world of *grandes courtisanes*. They haunted the *boîtes* and dance halls of Montmartre and were seldom of any fixed abode, unless it were some run-down brothel; but to all the world they had come to represent 'Gay Paree.' It was the company of which Yvette Guilbert sang with such incomparable art and understanding. The stratum of French life which Colette has transfixed forever in *Chéri* shows us a whole hierarchy of *grandes cocottes* who, well within living memory, were to be glimpsed, distractingly, across the ostrich boas and aigrettes at Maxim's, their first-water diamonds flashing in the last afterglow of agreeable dissipation. They lingered on, wasp-waisted, businesslike and daring, well into the early years of the twentieth century. But already they were retiring to properties at Biarritz, or Monte Carlo, and after the First World War, when the ranks of both international financiers and Russian Grand Dukes were so thinned, they were seen no more. They took with them not only a way of life, but the cumulative traditions of many centuries.

After World War II all the French establishments, both luxurious and sordid, were suppressed in a mood of purity hard to sustain; and it is indicative of the paucity, the economic pressure of this age that whether the ladies now operate in the shade or in the open, all of it — *grues, filles, trotteuses, belles de nuit, cocottes* — have now come to be known simply as *putes*. All the Gallic philosophy and tradition, all the nuances between an eighteenth-century Manon Lescaut, or a nineteenth-century Païa, all the inmates of a Maison Tellier, or a house in the rue Chabanais, have now been reduced by twentieth-century economics to *une putain*.

The leveling of society is reflected in this aspect of life, too. In the United States, which boasts less class distinction than elsewhere (income brackets apart), we now see an even greater simplification — that of the call girl. And here we might remark on the way in which the facility of American divorce tends to place some much-married ladies in the category of unofficial (or amateur) courtesans: though always with the spectre of alimony at the feast. In the early pioneer days, when the West was first opening up, there were flourishing chains of establishments, varying between brash saloons and log cabins. In San Francisco, women were such a rarity that a new arrival occasioned a journalistic review, in the manner now accorded a new play or book, where the lady's good and bad points were discussed in detail and a critical rating, usually of an indulgent nature, was given. By the late 1880s and 1890s, American sporting houses were world famous. Those of Chicago and New Orleans in particular developed a legendary quality and are immortalized in popular ballads. As the wealth of the young, vital nation accumulated, the demand for extravagant pleasures grew. (As George Sand wrote to: her daughter, Solange, 'Men with money to spend want women who know how to earn it.') So, while the come-by-chance fortunes of America were often being enjoyed by Diamond Lil and her rivals, there were champagne breakfasts and gold spittoons for the best clients, with perfumed fountains, four-piece orchestras scraping away tirelessly and, for very special occasions, clouds of live butterflies hovering gaudily. Today, in America, the courtesan may be said to have been replaced by the psychoanalyst. In place of the alcove there is the analyst's office. But basically the functions of both courtesan and analyst have the same principle. Both offer escape, relaxation and individual attention; both are expensive. And the couch is still there. *Plus ça change.*

2

Wellington taking leave of Harriette

HARRIETTE WILSON BELONGS to the Regency. She first appears on the scene about 1803 and disappears from it about 1825. During the Napoleonic wars England had turned inward upon itself, being even more isolated from Continental influences than before, (although it is known that no international tension ever prevented the Empress Josephine from receiving regular packages of English rose trees for her garden at Malmaison). And the fashionable set laced their talk with French phrases, a habit which Harriette's *Memoirs* reflect on every page. It was considered elegant to speak in a curious sort of half-and-half lingo.

It was an age of toughness, of brutal sports and crude practical jokes. Humour was coarse; wit steely. The noblemen, while retaining all the variety of affectations which they cultivated along with the manners of the jockeys and prize fighters with whom they consorted. The men about town, bucks, or Corinthians, rode like jockeys and boxed like professional pugilists. Lord Barrymore, a celebrated Corinthian, limped and was known as 'Cripplegate'; his two brothers, a disreputable pair, were 'Hellgate' and 'Newgate', (after the prison), while their sister was known s 'Billingsgate,' in reference to her language. One sporting dandy had his front teeth filed to points the better to whistle through them in the manner of the stagecoach drivers among whom he spent his days.

The diarist, Captain Gronow, writing in the 1860's, remembered the Regency dandies thus: 'How unspeakably odious — with a few brilliant exceptions such as Alvanley and others — were the dandies. They hated everybody and abused everybody and would sit together in White's bay window, or the pit boxes at the Opera, weaving tremendous crammers [tall stories]. They swore a good deal, never laughed, had their own particular slang, looked hazy after dinner, and had most of them been patronized at one time or another by Brummel and the Prince Regent.' Hunting, racing, horse breeding, cock-fighting, gambling for enormously high stakes, drinking themselves under the table, keeping a mistress such as Harriette, or Emma Hart — these were the diversions of Regency men of wealth and fashion.

They had little time, or inclination, to spare for women of breeding. They married them, begat heirs and occasionally escorted them to a Court Ball, or one of those evenings at Almack's, where to become a member; was almost equal to presentation at Court. Encouraged by the example of the Prince Regent, the First Gentleman of Europe, that glowing Prince Florizel who had, with time, become an obese, debauched figure, the butt of Rowlandson's most savage caricatures. Regency men considered it amusing to cuckold a friend or acquaintance. But in the main the women of their own station were neglected for a less exigent circle, such as that of Harriette Wilson and her sisters, 'the Fashionable Impures,' or Cyprians, as they were called. Among such women they could; forget current affectations and, for a while, be themselves. Although these men were lavish in their way of life — and their credit seemed inexhaustible — it was not so much on their women as on gambling and their stables that the largest sums of money were spent. Play ran very high at all the clubs along St. James's. Faro and macao were the favourite card games. At Crockford's the players wore a curious sort of wide-brimmed straw hat to shadow their faces, thus concealing any telltale emotions from the other players.

Bloodstock and extravagant equipages were another passion. Curricles, britzkas, tilburys and phaetons as high as a second-floor window skimmed about the streets like so many glittering, brilliant-coloured insects. Their line, carriage work and upholstery were triumphs of the carriage-maker's art. Generally the owner liked to drive himself. The bucks were famous for 'tooling the ribbons', or to continue their language, 'coming coachy in prime style.' They enjoyed dashing along the Bath, or Brighton, road driving a four- or six-in-hand, horse-whipping the turnpike men out of their way, overturning market carts and generally calling attention to their insufferable manners. They dressed themselves and their little 'tigers,' or grooms, to harmonize with the general turnout. Lord Petersham drove brown horses, had a brown carriage, wore a brown greatcoat and beaver hat, this serving, it was said, as a reminder of his unrequited passion for a beautiful widow of that name. Tommy Onslow, another celebrated buck, chose an all-black turnout and was criticized for looking like a hearse. But all of them paled beside a Mr. Cope, who was known as 'the Green Man.' His clothes, equipage and harness were all bright green; he powdered his hair green, was never seen to eat anything but spinach and was always accompanied by a poodle of greenish tinge.

In that age of individualists men were able not only to dress as they pleased but to live and love as they chose, besides ranging a whole field of amorous encounter, selecting a mistress of angelic or diabolic qualities and enjoying her for a night or a season in circumstances of anonymity or in the full glare of publicity. They were as personal, as exigent, in their choice of food. Lord Sefton, a great gourmet, employed Ude, the celebrated chef, at a considerable salary and undertook to leave him the same amount in an annual legacy, provided he retained his services to the end. But in such an age of individualism chefs too adopted a selective attitude. They were treated *en prince*; in some great houses the chef's name would be printed on the menu after the dish he had created, in the manner of a star performer. Carème, sure of his genius, declined to stay with no less a *bon viveur* than the Prince Regent. "His Royal Highness' cuisine is too bourgeois," he stated, and was joined by another chef who refused to follow his ducal master to Dublin since there was no opera there. Small wonder then, that Harriette, conquering this small world as she did, was a very remarkable creature.

London, as Harriette Wilson and her world knew it, comprised the small area of Mayfair, bounded on the north by Grosvenor Square, on the south by St. James's Park, on the east by Bond Street and on the west by Park Lane. Beyond the turnpike at Hyde Park Corner lay fields dotted with the villages of Chelsea, Brompton and Kensington. From Oxford Street, then known as the Oxford Road, there were uninterrupted vistas of Hampstead.

St. Paul's and the city lay outside the fashionable perimeter; they were for merchants and lawyers, just as the rookeries of St. Giles, Seven Dials and Drury Lane were for the cut-throats and drabs. The *ton*, or in-crowd, among whom Harriette moved, were all congregated in or around Mayfair. Some of the streets she knew and the houses where she lived still stand much as they did in her day. The little plum-red brick alleys of Shepherd Market, the sober elegance of Curzon Street, Chesterfield Street or Hertford Street are not greatly changed outwardly. In Charles Street, at No. 16, once the town house of the Earl of Craven, later the Guards Club, its splendid portals flanked by stone obelisks, Harriette's life of adventure might be said to have begun, if we are to believe the incomparable opening to her *Memoirs*. Here she is, recounting her fall:

> I shall not say why, or how, I became, at the age of
> fifteen, the mistress of the Earl of Craven. Whether it

was love, or the severity of my father, the depravity of my own heart, or the winning arts of the noble Lord, which induced me to leave my paternal roof and place myself under his protection, does not now much signify: or if it does, I am not in the humour to gratify curiosity in this matter.

Before that she had lived at her father's house. No. 23 Queen Street, a few doors away from No. 16 Charles Street. She and her sisters used to sit in the window of the family parlour, eyeing the mansion down the street; eyeing, too, the fine gentlemen who used to issue from its doorway and lounge down Queen Street with such a marked rallentando opposite No. 23. Presently Harriette kicked over the traces, dashed up the street to Lord Craven's arms and was never to return to her family again. But I anticipate.

In the London of that moment, oil lamps were only beginning to give place to gas lamps in 1816. In the obscurity crime flourished. Cut-throats, garrotters, pickpockets and street walkers abounded. There was no organized police force until 1820. The press gang struck terror wherever it went, seizing men for forced service in the navy. Malefactors were transported and sent to the dreaded hulks, or prison galleys were hanged at Tyburn or outside Newgate gaol, where huge crowds, which had paid high prices to get a place beside the scaffold, turned the matter into a sort of public holiday. Debtors were lodged at the Fleet or the Marshalsea Prison, where those who could afford to pay could still live in comfort, sending out for foods and wines and receiving their visitors alongside the more wretched, forgotten inmates. Lunatics were chained, existing in ghastly conditions at the Royal Bethlehem Hospital, where the public often repaired to observe their curious behaviour. Other diversions were Punch-and-Judy shows, raree-shows of performing fleas, or travelling fairs, with their mountebanks, wirewalkers and bearded women.

There were, besides, the circus, the theatre and the pleasure gardens at Vauxhall. The Argyle Rooms were celebrated for being the scene of an annual event, the Cyprians' Ball, given by the 'Fashionable Impures,' the demi-reps, who played hostess *en masse* to their admirers and protectors. In Cruikshank's drawing we see the sort of evening it was. Joy is obviously unrestrained; the ladies are waltzing giddily, offering their charms to whiskered oglers. Harriette, seen at the right, splendidly plumed, is on the arm of the publisher, Stockdale; her sister Amy, sitting below the cellist, displays a great deal too much leg. Bosoms, shoulders, all are for show, or for sale. In a contemporary account of the revels we are told that 'while the snowy orbs of nature undisguised heaved like the ocean with circling swell, the amorous lover palmed the melting fair and led her to where shame-faced Aurora … might hope in vain to draw aside the curtain and penetrate the mysteries of Cytherea.'

The writer goes on to say that in this territory of the Paphian Goddess, female invitations to the ball were confined to the stars and planets of the *demi-monde*. Distinguished personages of the other sex abounded, all the leading *roués* of the day being present. Listing 'the fair Dulcineas,' he speaks of The Venus Mendicant, The Mocking Bird, and Brazen Bellona, who, her father being a market gardener near Eton, had been launched on her career by the Etonians. Another, The White Doe, 'now reclines upon the velvet cushion of Independence,' while Laura, 'has money in the Funds.' In short, the assembled ladies represented the flower of their profession.

For the well-to-do, rather than the musical, there was the opera. This was regarded more as a fashionable promenade, or rendezvous, than as a musical entertainment, and for the men Court dress, knee breeches and *chapeaux bras* were *de rigueur*. Women of both the aristocracy and the *demi-monde* held court in their boxes each night; they eyed, and were eyed by, the whole house. To the demi-reps, to Harriette and her rivals, an opera box was a necessity — their showcase. Prices were high. For a box in the first tier, Harriette tells us, she paid 200 guineas a season, a considerable sum then and one which would today represent about £800.

Apart from the extreme luxury and sophistication of a small circle, London still retained much that was primitive in its tenor of life. Refuse accumulated and rotted in the gutters. Slops were flung from windows. The lack of any kind of hygiene was responsible for a high rate of infant mortality. It was not thought worthwhile to notify half the deaths; many were merely listed as being caused by 'convulsions'. In a city report about this time we read that o f the 21,780 deaths notified during the year, 4,809 were from consumption, largely due, no doubt, to the conditions of living half starved in overcrowded slums. There were 172 deaths in childbed, eleven from excessive drinking, (excessive eating was not mentioned, unless we count the 223 deaths from apoplexy). Cancer claimed only forty-two. The French pox, or syphilis, carried off sixty-five, leprosy two. The Thames being then used as a highway, 138 were drowned. There were five murders, 34 suicides, eight who were overlaid mysteriously, three who died of grief, as well as some deaths attributed to St. Anthony's Fire and 'the rising of the lights', which latter we must presume to have been a digestive complaint.

The apothecary dealt with minor ailments; teeth were still drawn at the street comer by itinerant quacks. The chiropodist, too, did a brisk, passing trade, taking up his pitch at a busy thoroughfare, brandishing his knife and scissors, crying "Corns to pick!" Most confinements were attended by the male midwife, reminiscent of Sterne's Dr. Slop. Harriette gives us a lively description of her sister Amy giving birth, presided over by Dr. Sam Merriman, in circumstances of great luxury provided by Amy's current protector and Harriette's former lover, the Duke of Argyll, who although in such a taking, (being then anxious to end the liaison and marry Lady Anglesey), performed all the rituals of an expectant father and ordered straw to be laid down before the house and the door knocker to be muffled at least three weeks before the birth. It was customary to speak of ladies in a delicate condition as being 'in the straw'.

There was little or no drainage system in the city; even the most commodious houses were only beginning to install water closets. Although these had been first introduced from Italy in the reign of Queen Elizabeth, they had not become popular, a chamber pot serving quite well enough for the next two centuries until water closets were at last reintroduced by Dr. Darwin, the biologist's grandfather. Beau Brummell was regarded as unbalanced in his passion for daily ablutions. His ritualistic morning toilet took upwards of five hours, one hour spent inching himself into his skin-tight buckskin breeches, an hour with the hairdresser and another two hours tying and 'creasing down' a series of starched cravats until perfection was achieved. But first of all two hours were spent scrubbing himself with fetish zeal from head to toe in milk, water and *eau de Cologne*. He was a close friend of Harriette's, though she tells us little of his idiosyncrasies. Beau Brummell said he used only the froth of champagne to polish his Hessian boots. He had 365 snuffboxes, those suitable for summer wear being quite unthinkable in winter, and the fit of his gloves was achieved by entrusting their cut to two firms — one for the fingers, the other for the thumbs. Sometimes, however, the tyranny of elegance became altogether insupportable. A Mr. Boothby committed suicide and left a note saying he could no longer endure the *ennui* of buttoning and unbuttoning.

The niceties of masculine fashion seem to have taken precedence over female fashion at this time. No doubt there were elegant women and dowdy ones, but man was the *arbiter elegantiarum* of the age. Military uniforms reached a degree of brilliance that belied their wearers' martial spirit. The officers of the Guards were wont to shelter their splendours under umbrellas, even on the field of battle, unless engaged in particularly active combat. But this practice was finally proscribed by the Duke of Wellington in his Peninsular campaign, during a season of torrential rains.

Both Wellington and Napoleon were eminently practical men. They knew there was a time for dressing-up and a time for undressing too. I am reminded of the anecdote told by Wellington to his confidante, Mrs. Arbuthnot, on the methods Napoleon wished to employ in order to distract the Parisian public's attention from the appalling losses in the Russian campaign then in progress. He ordered that the ballet dancers at the opera were to appear *sans culotte*. The order was given, but the dancers flatly refused to comply. 'Wellington added,' says Mrs. Arbuthnot in her journal, 'that if the women had consented he did not doubt but that it would have obliterated all recollection of the Russian losses. Wellington was categorical. "This anecdote," he said, "he knew for a fact".' The Iron Duke had a sound understanding of human nature. He was being realistic, rather than cynical, when, during the Peninsular campaigns he set a limit of forty-eight hours for an officer's leave in Lisbon, or behind the lines. This, he said, was as long as any reasonable man could wish to spend in bed with any woman.

While the Prince Regent and Beau Brummell led masculine fashion, the ladies of the royal family — the Prince's retiring mother, Queen Charlotte, and her stodgy daughters — lived withdrawn. The wives and mistresses of his brothers, too, did not set up to be *élégantes*. In his choice of mistresses, such as Lady Hertford, or Lady Conyingham, the Prince always showed an irresistible attraction for maturity bordering on the elderly. When Lady Conyingham was first installed as the favourite, the diarist Greville notes that Lord Beauchamp, a cynical young peer, encountered her riding in the park with her royal lover, which caused him to say, "By God, our grandmother will have to learn to ride or it will be all up with us."

There were some women's magazines, such as *La Belle Assemblée*, which printed coloured fashion plates inspired by Paris, where mantua-makers, milliners, perfumiers, glove and shoemakers advertised their wares. Advertisements dwelled on the merits of 'long stays which compass into form the chaos of the flesh.' We read of all kinds of cushions, plumpers and padded rolls to hide defects, though of these Harriette could have had no need. There are frequent references to her lovely figure, her small waist and voluptuous bosom. Paint was lavishly used: red, black and white; a primitive palette. There were fearful concoctions of white lead and vegetable rouge and, only a generation back, one of the lovely Gunning sisters had died of lead poisoning induced by the excessive use of cosmetics.

Dental skill being in its infancy, teeth were either good or bad. False teeth were an expensive luxury, and we are told that Mrs. Fitzherbert's charms were much impaired by an ill-fitting set. Different ages have different standards of conduct, and beauty too. Small hands and feet were one of the first essentials of beauty to nineteenth-century Europe. From the Thames to the Neva, poets were intoxicated by glimpses o f their mistresses' tiny feet. Oddly, this standard seems to have been applied to men too. There are frequent references in Harriette's *Memoirs* to the 'small, white, soft' hands of the men upon whom she dotes. Lord Byron and Lord Ponsonby are both described as having 'little hands'.

Judging by the portraits of the period — particularly the Dighton series of celebrated London personalities, many of them Harriette's protectors or friends — we see that even the young were of a portly inclination. Lord Alvanley, choked into a high, starched stock, a beaver hat crammed down on his wine-flushed face, is the perfect image of a Regency buck, but he wears his weight well. And his wit was airy. Creevey called him a natural wag. Greville found him the delight and ornament of society, but O'Connell, with whom he fought a duel, called him a bloated buffoon. He lived high, and once ordered a dish which cost him £108. He was partial to cold apricot tart, which he insisted on having on his side table

every day, all the year round. Continuing the fashionable cult of individualism, he liked to read in bed but not to blow out the candle. Therefore, he would hurl the candle on to the floor; if it still burned he would fling a pillow at it. This reckless arrogance recalls Lord Cardigan, (of the Light Brigade), who, when pick-nicking in his carriage, always flung the tray with all its luxurious silver, glasses and porcelain, out of the carriage window, saying it was the only way to picnic without a mess. Arrogance was inbred in these men. They were patricians and intended to avail themselves of every privilege which their birth accorded them and their wealth obtained.

Even the great Wellington, always far removed from the more spectacular follies of his age, reveals an unconscious hauteur and a contempt for both progress and the masses when he dismisses the new steam railway as 'a project which would encourage the lower classes to move about needlessly'. This same mixture of imperiousness and common sense, this sureness of themselves which was ever a fundamental characteristic of the British aristocracy, is found again, years later, when the Duke, an old man, admonishes the young heiress, Angela Burdett-Coutts, twenty-five and deeply in love with him. Casting discretion to the winds, she visited him unaccompanied and wished to plunge into an entanglement. 'My dearest,' writes the Duke, 'I tell you very firmly I will not allow it. I did not think you would be guilty of such folly'. He goes on to remind her that she will be still young when he is a wreck. What supreme confidence is shown here by the old general, still so shrewd, so vital, so sure of himself as a man! 'I entreat you again, in this way, not to throw yourself away upon a Man old enough to be your Grandfather, who, however Strong, Hearty and Healthy at present, must and will certainly *in time*' [the italics are mine] 'feel the consequences and infirmities of Age.' Even at seventy, the Duke spoke of infirmity and age as a melancholy prospect rather than an existing fact.

3

The Marquis of Worcester lacing
Harriette Wilson's stays etc

H ARRIETTE'S *MEMOIRS* ARE very personal; they do not reflect the larger aspects of her age as do those of the classic diarists, Creevey, Greville, or Gronow. There is some mention of the Napoleonic wars, since many of her *beaux* saw action in the various campaigns, and Wellington himself was one of them. But of outstanding events, whether Nelson's death in 1805, the first performance of a Mozart opera in England, at His Majesty's Theatre in 1806, Pitt's abolition of Slavery, or the Congress of Vienna, we hear nothing. Bonaparte is mentioned only once.

London has always consisted of a series of overlapping but completely separate quarters. The *ton*, or in-crowd, living in Mayfair, found it impossible to envisage anything farther east than the Haymarket. Beau Brummell spoke for all of them when, in reply to an invitation to dine in Bloomsbury, he accepted, 'providing my coachman can find his way there'. Literary London — that is, the successful and fashionable authors — all congregated at 50 Albemarle Street, then, the beautiful premises of the publishing firm of John Murray. "My Murray," says Byron, who treated the place as his club, bank, home and refuge from the more importunate ladies, such as Caroline Lamb. Here, in the red drawing room, he used to meet with all the men of letters of the day, and when Harriette Wilson tried to crash these gates and set up in authorship, she could never forgive Mr. Murray's unenthusiastic behaviour. One of Harriette's rivals, Julia Johnstone, insisted that Harriette's culture was mere affectation, since she and her sisters were nourished on Monk Lewis and Mrs. Radcliffe's horrific novels … 'I have often written out quotations from Shakespeare and Milton and others for Harriette to use in conversation'. And from the same source we learn that Harriette's literary aspirations led her, not only to quote Shakespeare, but to write a farce which she herself took very seriously, and submitted to John Kemble. But it seems this manuscript met with no better success than the one she offered to Mr. Murray.

A less successful literary group was formed at Euston where, in an atmosphere vibrant with passions and higher thought, Mary Wollstonecraft, author of *Vindication of the Rights of Women*, had lived with her husband, Godwin, and where their daughter grew into the gentle, unhappy idealist who was to marry Shelley and write *Frankenstein*. The pompous city merchants were centred around Bloomsbury. Somers Town was a favourite neighbourhood for the Cyprians of second rank, who were installed there, in comfort if not in style, by their lovers. It was conveniently removed from Mayfair, yet easy of access. Harriette Wilson lived there for a short while in her early days when under the protection of Fred Lamb, and prior to engaging the affections of the Duke of Argyll, then Marquis of Lorne, who soon removed her to Argyll House, Mayfair, and fame.

All these changes of house, or lover, are recorded with candour, though perhaps not always with accuracy. Harriette has a fine disregard for exactitude, either in names, places or dates. Incidents which most likely occurred, are set wildly, some years out of date. Wellington is referred to the Duke some years before he obtained that title. The Duke of Argyll, who during their liaison was Marquis of Lorne, is called both Lorne and 'Argyle'. The Marquis of Hertford is sometimes Lord Yarmouth. Harriet and Byron discuss Lady Caroline Lamb's *roman à clef, Glenarvon*, several years before it is published — that is, if they discussed it at Wattier's Masquerade, as she says. But does it signify? Dates make ladies nervous: stories dry, says Harriette — no lady and never dry.

The *Memoirs* may be said to derive directly from the sixth Duke of Beaufort. We must always be grateful. Without his stinginess, without the backsliding of his son and heir, the Marquis of Worcester, we might never have had them. When, some years earlier, Worcester was at his height of his passion for Harriette, to whom he was in the habit of writing the most imprudent promises of marriage, addressed to his adored 'wife', his 'angelick' Harriette, he was kept from the altar only by the fact that he had not reached his majority and, Harriette assures us, by her refusal, her positive refusal, to become a Marchioness. Be that as it may, the Duke and Duchess of Beaufort began to grow very uneasy after two years of their son's spectacular constancy. Every effort was made to separate the lovers without success. Presently the Duke's lawyers approached Harriette, offering her a sum of money for the return of Lord Worcester's letters. Harriette's own lawyer advised her they were worth about £20,000, but Harriette, incurably sentimental, wished to get on good terms with her lover's family. She returned most of the letters, (though retaining enough worldly sense to hold some back), and wrote an affecting letter saying her only wish was to be considered more kindly by the Beauforts. Naturally this remained unanswered.

The Duke now succeeded in having his son ordered off to the wars. He was to join Wellington's staff in the Peninsula. Lord Worcester spoke of suicide. Tears streamed down his cheeks. Harriette began to feel she had perhaps set too little value on the young man's passion. Grief ruled the day; the lovers could hardly be parted for an hour during the last weeks together. Indeed, Lord Worcester's uncle was dispatched to drag him from Harriette's arms and see him aboard the ship for Spain. Meantime Harriette undertook to remain true to her love, (on a modest allowance provided by the family lawyers). Lord Worcester was a splendid catch. Young, ardent, romantic, his beaky parrot nose spoke of his Plantaganet and FitzRoy ancestry, while his quarterings displayed the *fleur-de-lis* of France and the lion of England. His father was the sixth Duke of Beaufort. The family had always been closely associated with the Crown. Their name recurs nobly throughout English history and their historic home, Badminton, was only one of several splendid estates. After all, Harriette might have argued, was she really aiming too high? There was the case of Mary Anne Clarke who, with no more pretensions to beauty or breeding than Harriette, had been set up by H.R.H. the Duke of York, brother of the Prince of Wales, the Duke having agreed to pay Mrs. Clarke £1,000 a month. On this understanding the lady had filled her stables with bloodstock, kept twenty servants, including three chefs, and never ate off anything but gold or silver plate. 'Gay goings-on in Gloucester Place,' says a contemporary before Mary Anne Clarke found that, due to her allowance being paid to her so very irregularly, she was obliged to traffic in military appointments and preferments, this course being made easy for her as the Duke of York was Commander-in-Chief of the British Army. This eventually led to her public examination in the House of Commons on a charge of corruption. She was by then a fallen favourite. But this did not happen till 1809. When Harriette was discomforting the Beaufort family Mary Anne Clarke was still supreme, an object lesson in triumphant depravity. So Harriette held out for her marquis and the Beauforts placed their faith in time and distance.

The better to avoid those snares of fashionable society of which Lord Worcester was so apprehensive, Harriette promised to bury herself in a village in Devon. She was to spend a year there, awaiting her lover's majority. Upon which, it was agreed between them that she should join him in Spain and nothing on earth should prevent the marriage. But reading between the lines, we see that life in the country, for Harriette, was no life at all. 'She had no idea of ruralizing, she was a real city madam,' says Julia who, according to her *Confessions*, shared Harriette's exile, and even endeavoured to restrain her friend's exuberance. 'Once,' she says, 'Harriette nearly betrayed her calling as we were going to church, by holding up her leg on a passing stile and desiring the clergyman to fasten her bootlace. He had once been a dasher on the London streets and very gallantly complied with her request, saying with a smile, "Don't your garters want tightening, my love?" I could have brained her with my fan,' adds the refined Julia.

Even with such diversions, Harriette chafed. Since the Beaufort lawyers were always in arrears with her allowance, she decided to have done with dullness and Devon. She wrote to Worcester and agreed to join him without further delay. Alas, she had gone no farther than Falmouth, where she was awaiting the packet-boat, when news reached her of Lord Worcester's infatuation with a paymaster's wife. It was not to be borne. She returned to London and her former ways.

High dramas ensued, which the *Memoirs* relate in full. When threatened with a breach of promise case the Beaufort family were prompt with their payments. But when they tried to wriggle out of their undertakings by offering a cash settlement of £1,200 down, Harriette's ire was roused. On the advice of no less an advocate than Lord Brougham, she says, set took the Duke to court and would have won her case had not Lord Worcester stepped in and revealed that by certain letters she had written him from Devonshire she had broken her side of the agreement. Thus, on her late lover's evidence, Harriette lost her case. Gradually she from fashion, her looks faded and she had to accept second-rate men and second-rate terms. She moved to Paris around 1815 and for the first time a note of lasting melancholy creeps into the *Memoirs*. She learned, now, to be content with tawdry triumphs. Most of her old friends were marrying, or forgetting her determinedly. She was not of much consequence in Paris, and we sense with what eagerness she welcomes the few Englishmen whom she encounters. But, as she says, 'it won't do to play the game of hearts in Paris'.

4

*Harriette Wilson and party
at the Marquis of Hereford's*

THERE IS A silence of some years before we hear of her, now really hard pressed for money, and under the influence of the disreputable Colonel Rochfort, welcoming the publisher Stockdale's scheme for producing her *Memoirs* in a manner most calculated to bring the biggest returns. As been remarked, Harriette was not by nature spiteful; she seldom bore malice. But here, we feel, she fell in with Stockdale with a special gusto. It must have been a great pleasure to discomfort the Beaufort family once more; they had treated her very shabbily. And Lord Worcester, now suitably married, presented a perfect target. I think it likely that the *Memoirs* would never have been written had she been able to settle down into a snug middle age on a Beaufort pension.

Harriette now circularized all her former friends and lovers, advising them of her intentions. Two hundred pounds down by return of post was her price of omission from the *Memoirs*, and she kept her word. "We imagine with what alarm such letters were received, an alarm tinged with exasperation, since Harriette was in the habit of sealing her letters with her own seal or device. One bore the message *Andante Felice* — go in happiness; another, with the image of a cupid, bore one word — 'Hush'! Their irritant qualities, in the present circumstances were not lost on Harriette, we feel. It must have added to the fun. Many apprehensive gentlemen paid up by return, and felt it well worthwhile. Some braved great flourish by Joseph Stockdale, a 'Caliban figure' lurking in the shady purlieu of the Opera Colonnade, off the Haymarket, where a besieging mob had to be held back by barricades, so overwhelming was the demand for the first instalment. St. James's was in a ferment. Boodles, Crockford's, White's — the sober façade of each club concealed an uproar. The noble members, now come into their honours and titles, ministers of the Crown, married, fathers of families, setting into a triumphant maturity, found themselves pilloried, their callow follies, their passions and weaknesses displayed with a ruthless objectivity. Once again, we feel that Harriette was enjoying her work.

It would seem that she chose her moment well. Just as she had led the unfettered, hedonistic life of her inclination during the Regency, so now, at its close, she found, with her decline, the perfect moment to extract a price for her silence. Times had changed. Yet even twenty years earlier that England which had countenanced so many follies and excesses, and had accepted the lovely dissolute Emma Hart becoming not only Lady Hamilton but British Ambassadress at the Court of Naples, could not countenance her being bequeathed to the nation by the nation's hero, Nelson. Lady Hamilton and Horatia, her child by Lord Nelson, were left to perish. Even in 1805 a line was drawn between private life and public gestures.

From Creevey we learn that Mrs. Fitzherbert, who was the Prince Regent's mistress and probably his wife, was also opposed to Lady Hamilton's influence. The Prince was greatly affected by the news of Lord Nelson's death, 'but Mrs. Fitzherbert at once entered into an account of the domestic failings of Lord Nelson, in a way infinitely creditable to her'.

We visualize the scene: the portly Prince, fidgety but respectful while Mrs. Fitzherbert pronounced, his bulging eyes straying sometimes beyond the green lawns of the Pavilion to the Steine gardens, where fair passers-by were glimpsed beyond the flowerbeds that bordered the royal residence. Mrs. Fitzherbert was entirely for Lady Nelson, we learn. Lady Hamilton, she said, 'overpowered Lord Nelson, hero though he was, and took possession of him quite by force ...' But in 1806 the Prince fell desperately in love with Lady Hertford and Mrs. Fitzherbert's censure was of no more consequence.

There followed a few more years of latitude before respectability took over with growing momentum. By the time Harriette struck, twenty years later, the effect was cataclysmic. London society spoke of nothing else; pirated editions appeared rapidly, and broadsheets, crudely illustrated, were sold in the thousands. There were the most entertaining pictures of the Marquis of Worcester lacing Harriette Wilson's stays with one hand and toasting her breakfast bread with the other. There were pictures of Harriette pursuing Lord Ponsonby, and of Lord Deerhurst accosting her sister Sophia. No one was immune. Sir Walter wrote in his journal, 'The gay world has been kept in hot water lately by the impudent publication of the celebrated Harriot Wilson, who lived with half the gay world at hack and manger, and now obliges such as will not pay hush money with a history of whatever she knows or invents about them.' Scott conceded 'she has some good retailing of conversations, in which the style of the speaker, so far as known to me, is exactly imitated'. It was this very quality which made the *Memoirs* so unpalatable, so unforgivable, to many of her former friends.

The manner in which Stockdale announced each successive instalment was calculated to obtain the maximum attention. Encouraged by the success of the opening numbers, he announced the next in these terms:

Part VII will be ready on Monday, 4th April, at 2 o'clock precisely and Part VIII on Monday, 18th April, at the same hour.

Preceding this there had been a statement intended to arouse alarm and the most lively curiosity. The noble persons mentioned in *Memoirs* had been listed like an inventory. Under the heading *Exhibits in Parts IV, V and VI* he had announced:

Dukes: Argyll, Beaufort (and Duchess), de Guiche, Leinster, Weillington.
Marquesses: Anglesea, Bath, Headfort, Sligo, Worcester …

and so on down, through Earls, Barons, Honourables, to Colonels, Captains and even the modest Esquire. An equal treat was promised with the forthcoming instalments.

For some while Harriette had been sending each successive instalment through the bag — the Foreign Office official valise. When the new Ambassador to France turned out to be none other than that pompous Lord Granville whom Harriette had tried out and found wanting on the hot, long walk to Hampstead and back so many years ago, he quickly put a stop to the practice. But he had not reckoned with Harriette, who wrote telling him that she had been looking about for a fool to fill up her *Memoirs* and that he had presented himself just in time.

The whole affair engendered a great deal of unpleasantness and more and more gentlemen now took almost permanent refuge in their clubs where, among themselves, Harriette's victims discussed how best to defend themselves against her onslaughts. The Hon. Edward 'Bear' Ellice, M.P. for Invergarry, Secretary to the Treasury, a wealthy man owning vast estates in Canada, was one of those who had no intention of paying Harriette's price. On receiving a letter from her, he published it in an effort to unite action against her. Here is Harriette, impertinent and impenitent:

> *Paris. 111 Rue du Faubourg*
> *St. Honoré,*
> *March 8, 1825.*

Sir —

People are buying themselves so fast out of my book, 'Memoirs of HarrietteWilson,' that I have no time to attend to them. Sh'd be sorry not to give each a chance if they chuse to be out.You are quizzed most unmercifully.Two Noble Dukes have taken my word and I have never named them. I am sure _____ wd say you might trust me not to publish or cause to he published aught about you if you like to forward £200 directly to me, else it will he too late as the last volume in which you shine will be the property of the Editor, and in his hands. Lord _____ [name removed by Ellice] says he will answer for aught I agree to, and so will my husband. Do just as you like. Consult only yourself. I get as much for a small book as you will give me for taking you out, or more. I attack no poor men because they cannot help themselves. Adieu! — Mind, I have no time to write again, as what with writing books and then altering them for those who buy out, I am done up — frappé en mort.What do you think of my French ?

> Yours, H. ROCHFORT, late Wilson
> *P.S. Don't trust the bag with your answer.*

It is sometimes said that Lord Ponsonby, (Harriette's great love), owed the start of his diplomatic career to the fact that he had given Harriette some of his old love letters, notably those of Lady Conyingham, once his mistress and now George IV's favourite. Harriette threatened to publish these letters, it is alleged. But Prime Minister Canning settled things by nominating Ponsonby Ambassador to a new capital, Buenos Aires, thus removing him from Harriette's reach and from Lady Conyingham's too, which greatly relieved the King, jealous to distraction over his inamorata. In any case, nothing more was ever heard of the letters and Lord Ponsonby's diplomatic career kept him out of England for many years.

The Duke of Wellington was one of those who refused to be exploited. With the same vigour and dispatch with which he once sought Hariette's embraces he is said to have sent back her demands with the famous phrase 'Publish and be damned' scrawled across it in red ink. In his daily walks and talks with his confidante, Mrs. Arbuthnot, he had to explain that it had all been a very long time ago, that he doubted that he would ever recognize Harriette if he saw her now. Mrs. Arbuthnot noted it all down in her journal and seemed quite satisfied.

Not so Harriette. It would never do if men began to brave it out. It is not surprising, therefore, that the Duke cuts a rather poor figure in the *Memoirs*. This was Harriette's method of revenging herself on those who did not co-operate. 'Men are more hurt at being painted weak silly creatures than gross blackguards,' she wrote *à propos* of her methods of extortion, and we see the Iron Duke, Marquis of Douro, Field Marshal of Great Britain, Duke of Ciudad Rodrigo, Prince of Waterloo in the Netherlands, and so many more titles besides, as a faintly comic character 'looking,' she said, 'rather like a rat-catcher'. Even so, something of his essential largeness — his generosity and chivalresque attributes — emerges from the pages. However Harriette chooses to present her subjects, it must be agreed she has an acute, Dickensian sense of character. No doubt it was convenient for her subjects to denounce the *Memoirs* as a tissue of lies. Yet, inaccurate or no, a ring of most unmistakable truth pervades the whole, and where I have ventured to cut the enormous original, it is only to avoid the more repetitious or padded passages.

Harriette Dubochet — for Wilson she chose as her professional name, (it never seems to have been associated with any of her protectors) — was born in London, in Mayfair, on 2 February, 1786, 'at ten minutes before 8 o/c'. This date is almost the only one in all her life of which we are sure. She was christened in the parish church of St. George's, Hanover Square, as the daughter of John Dubochet and Amelia Cook, his wife. They lived in a little house; No. 2 Carrington Street, Shepherd Market, now vanished.

There were fifteen children. Of the nine who survived, only three of the girls followed the path of virtue. Mary and Diana, whom Harriette speaks of as Paragon, and the youngest, Charlotte, appear seldom in the Memoirs. They lived in retired, or domestic, circumstances far removed from the raffish society frequented by Harriette. (Creevey makes one mysterious reference: 'Lord Lascelles' son has married Harriette Wilson's sister,' he writes in 1819. Which sister? Nothing in the Lascelles family bears out Creevey's statement.)

Amy, the eldest, a dark-eyed virago, Fanny, a golden creature for whom no one ever had a harsh word, Harriette, and their younger sister, Sophia, who set out to copy her sisters' way of life and bagged Lord Deerhurst at thirteen — all were stylish courtesans. But with this difference: while the legendary charmers of history, the hetaerae, the geishas and most of the more celebrated courtesans of other ages lived in an atmosphere of mystery, as high priestesses of seduction, the Dubochet sisters retained a cosy and most down-to-earth simplicity. Their amours were set less, it seems, in the voluptuous decor of the alcove, such as French eighteenth-century engravings have immortalized, (those inviting little supper-tables set beside a canopied bed, tumbled with curtains, laces and discarded chemises), than in a setting at once more brisk and matter-of-fact — at a coaching inn on the Bath Road maybe, or in one of those snug little dun-brick London houses which still abound between Bond Street and the Park.

We read of a very pressing suitor shown into Harriette's parlour just as the cloth was being laid for supper; of Lord Berwick hurling a leg of mutton at the footman's head. Amy entertains the dandies, the *beau monde*, the *emigré* French princes of the Blood and all the diplomatic corps at her little love nest in York Place, the tiny, narrow hallway and stairs crammed with fine gentlemen, the upstairs drawing room wedged with half Burke's Peerage. She feeds them cold chicken, washed down by claret and champagne. But it goes against the grain. Amy is mean; she herself is nourished on black pudding, a rather unromantic dish which she endeavours to conceal from her elegant patrons. Sophia, a glum girl, 'dumb' in modem parlance, is dispatched by Amy to fetch home this plebeian sausage and suffers agonies of mortification when, seeing Lord Deerhurst approaching, she vainly tries to dispose of the black pudding in the gutter and it is returned to her by a passer-by. These are homely incidents, and it was perhaps these very natural qualities which made the Dubochet sisters so irresistible to the men of fashion, who had to spend so much time maintaining standards of excessive artificiality if they wished to follow the tone set by Beau Brummell.

Above all, the Dubochet sisters must have been good company. We long to have known them. Across the century-and-a-half that separates us, we catch echoes of the chatter, the murmurs of admiration, the gaiety and the bursts of laughter which accompanied them wherever they went. These lusty young creatures, so full of life, so amoral, so frankly enjoying themselves, must have been delicious to know. It is impossible to imagine a dull moment in their society. If not beautiful, they were alluring, with that special allure of the woman who knows she is desired by many. They were elegant, had cultivated graces; they were good linguists and musicians; they could discuss politics and current literature as well as newest scandal. They were witty, improvident, imprudent — and to be had. The mixture must have been irresistible.

Alas, they missed being photographed by a mere thirty-five years. If only we could see them, fixed forever, smiling out at us from the opaque shadows of a daguerreotype! The earliest tintypes give us a sense of verity no portrait can. The turn of a neck, the curve of a hand, an expression in the eyes — these things are irrefutable in a photograph, however faded and stiff. By 1840 Fox-Talbot was posing those quiet family groups on the lawns of Laycock Abbey. Only thirty-five years separate us from the possibility of gazing today at a laughing group of girls — Amy, Fanny, Harriette, Julia and Sophia.

Harriette was the most successful of all the sisters, unless we allow that Sophia, by marrying Lord Berwick and withdrawing to propriety and Leamington Spa, succeeded better. Harriette was the rage. All fashionable London aspired to be her lover for a night or two, or her protector for longer, or, at least, to be one of the crowd who jammed themselves into the opera box where she held court, levelling her glasses across the house, fancying this man or that, quizzing the pit and the parterre. "Pray send your patting men to me," says Mrs. Julia Johnstone, her rival, to Amy, who always professes innocence yet claims to have been able to obtain £100 at will, merely by allowing a Mr. Hart Davis to pat her arm. Not that Harriette would have been contented with pats. It must be admitted that she took a most unprofessional delight in her calling. Although the *Memoirs* arc neither pornographic, nor even erotic, in the sense of the writings of Casanova, or Paul de Kock, yet sandwiched between her pawky accounts of daily life (her daily life making, it must be remembered, very racy reading) arc passages which disclose besides her roaring appetites ('not that I love a saint, but something which is most luxuriously sly and quiet ...') her passionate love for Lord Ponsonby.

This affair was to shadow all the rest of her life. It was to her something which transcended mere mortal bliss. Writing to Lord Byron fifteen years after it was all over, she says, 'Don't despise me, nothing Lord Ponsonby has dearly loved can be vile, or destitute, of merit.' Ponsonby was, to her, a man apart; a god. She speaks of her sufferings when he terminated the relationship as mortal agony. She who loved life, men and love, and had so much of all three did, I believe, centre the whole force of her emotion on Ponsonby. After he had gone there was shadow and sunlight, money to be earned, appetites to be gratified, bills to be paid, a losing battle to be fought courageously against ill-health and age — but never again the bright chimera of love as she had known it centred in him. Still, she had dwelled with the rose.

In the beginning, about 1799, when she and her sisters used to sit in the window of the Dubochet home in Queen Street, times were hard and the girls passed as stocking menders. Their mother, whom Harriette adored, seems to have been a gentle and loving parent. Her business of Stocking Repairs flourished at that moment, for knee breeches were still generally worn and went out of fashion only around 1820. Unkind tongues hinted that Mrs. Dubochet had also followed the profession her daughters later embraced. But she is also said to have been the illegitimate child o f a country squire, adopted and brought up in loving kindness by a Mr. and Mrs. Cook, stocking menders by trade, from whom the little Amelia obtained her surname and her skill at darning. When she married Dubochet, the Swiss watchmaker, twenty years her senior, he made some pretence of earning, being employed in the office of a coal wharf, but for the most part he was absorbed in mathematical calculations and accepted his wife's earnings unquestioningly. He appears to have been a detestable character, a domestic tyrant, violent-tempered, and one in whom his family, not unnaturally, did not confide. The only occasion when he sounds human is when his youngest daughter, Sophia, marries Lord Berwick and he is able to preen it over a patronizing neighbour. He came from the canton of Berne and was said, though not by Harriette, to be the child of that Elizabeth Dubochet who had been seduced by Lord Chesterfield and who was the mother of his son, Philip, to whom he addressed his celebrated *Letters*.

There is one highly-coloured account of his ancestry which describes how a Mlle. Debouchette, a lovely young creature, a *limonadière* at the Hague, attracted the attention of a party of profligate English noblemen — the Earl of Chesterfield among them. She resisted all his advances until, at last, determined to win a bet on the subject, he adopted a course of action suggested by his Italian valet, no doubt an expert in such matters. A carriage was stationed nearby while the Earl and his valet held a lighted sheet, saturated with spirits, at her window, crying fire. When she rushed out they seized her and made off with her to the coach. Her brother challenged Lord Chesterfield since he refused to marry his victim. But, having settled a considerable sum of money on her, he was at last permitted to take her to England. There she lived under Chesterfield's protection, in discreet retirement at Chelsea, where Harriette Wilson's father was born. With such animated parental backgrounds on both sides it is not surprising that, one by one, the lovely Dubochet sisters left home to set up for themselves.

Amy went first, and, having decided to walk about London till she met her destiny, she accepted a Mr. Trench for no other reason than it seemed difficult to refuse him longer than two days. He was succeeded by General Madden and then Mr. Sydenham, by whose name she was generally known. But there were many other interludes — with the *Corps Diplomatique* in particular. Counts Benckendorff, the Duke of Palmella and others. In her forties, Amy married an Italian harpist, Signor Bochsa who behaved very badly to her and was a most unsatisfactory husband.

Fanny was the next to go; she had many adorers but seems to have been steadily under the protection of the Marquis of Hertford, Lord Yarmouth or 'Red Herrings' in his younger days. Colonel Parker was her undoing. They set up an establishment together and Fanny — gentle, pretty, kindly Fanny — believed she had found peace. The Colonel wished her to be known as Mrs. Parker. She was treated with great respect by all his fellow officers and he seems to have accepted unquestioningly the presence of George, her son by an earlier liaison. But after a few years of this quasi-domestic bliss, Colonel Parker coolly announced he was about to be married. Fanny never recovered from the blow. Complaining of a pain in her heart, she withdrew from the world, pined and faded. Her last hours were made easier by the kindness of Lord Hertford, whom Thackeray has painted as the profligate Marquis of Steyne in *Vanity Fair*. He had moved to the then rustic freshness of Brompton Road and himself rushed to Piccadilly and back at the gallop to fetch her *eau-de-Cologne*. But no one could bring back Colonel Parker. Fanny sank and died, one summer evening, in Harriette's arms.

However, before that melancholy end, there were a number of years, from about the beginning of the century to 1815, when the three sisters swam in an aura of gaiety and adventure. Harriette soon followed her two elder sisters, starting out, according to the *Memoirs*, at fifteen as Lord Craven's mistress. Later she was followed by Sophia, an early starter, at thirteen. Although they all remained on close terms, the atmosphere was often charged with vituperation; they confided in one another, borrowed one another's clothes and poached on one another's preserves. Amy, or Mrs. Sydenham, was always a little removed. Less successful, she was jealous and unscrupulous. She was constantly trying to acquire her sisters' more spectacular conquests and sometimes succeeded. Fanny, Harriette and their friend and rival, Julia Johnstone, were known as the Three Graces, while Amy was unkindly known as one of the Furies. All of them took a sisterly interest in Sophia and gave her much advice which, however, she does not seem to have needed, for she very soon persuaded Lord Berwick to marriage and from her rarefied position as a peeress snubbed, patronized and finally ignored her family. Sir Walter Scott relates that at the opera Harriette's box was directly above that of Lady Berwick, and Harriette used occasionally to remind her reformed sister of her presence by spitting on her head.

Julia Johnstone occupies a special place in these pages, for not only was she a professional friend and rival of Harriette's but she has left her *Confessions* in which she has sought to vilify Harriette and to give us other accounts of the events which Harriette records. Her version of Harriette's beginnings is very different from that cited in the *Memoirs*. Julia Johnstone writes spitefully; she is of no weight, and is far more inaccurate than Harriette. For example, she flatly states that Harriette was never regularly under Lord Worcester's protection, but that she was sometimes favoured with his attentions. This was patently said to denigrate Harriette's charms, or the rank of her lovers. Yet in the correspondence between Lady Bessborough and Lord Granville Leveson-Gower, dated 24 September, 1813, we read: 'Harriette Wilson is living at Ryde in great retirement, she passes for the most Virtuous Woman in the Island; she is waiting for Lord W.'s coming of age when he is to return and marry her. She shew'd some of his letters, all ending with yr affecn Husband ...' As Lord Granville was the Duchess of Beaufort's brother, Lady Bessborough was no doubt only reporting a situation which was already causing lively anxiety in the Beaufort family.

Still, I quote Julia's *Confessions* at some length, since they form a sort of counterpoint by which the reader sees two opposing views, or accounts, of events and people.

Mrs. Johnstone was a charmer whose languid, high-bred manners concealed a most sensuous nature. Twelve children were the fruits of her passions, and when she loved it was with overwhelming solemnity. She was ahead of her time; already in Julia we sense that Victorian cant so far from the roaring Regency mood. For a while she and Harriette were inseparables. Although Harriette's *Memoirs* seldom miss a chance to diminish Julia's charms, it is with an offhanded, good-natured patronage rather than with the cold fury Julia reserves for Harriette. When the *Memoirs* were first published, Julia reappeared from the shadows. Harriette had categorically stated that Julia was dead and that she, Harriette, had visited her on her deathbed. But a most lively shade returned: languor had given place to rage. Within two months of the *Memoirs'* publication Julia rushed into print with *The True Confessions of Julia Johnstone, written by herself, in contradiction to the Fables of Harriette Wilson.* They fell very flat. Even then it was seen that she was activated by purely personal motives. She wished to whitewash herself and pour venom and scorn, however late, on her one-time rival. Her description of Fanny's death is savage, she attributes it to drink. 'She screamed to live and had no hope of a; blessed hereafter; I fear it may prove a family deathbed,' she says, at once unctuous and cruel.

Her description of Harriette at forty is as cruel, but probably more exact. 'Imagine to yourself a little woman in a black beaver hat and long grey cloak. No tightening at the waist to show the figure of the wearer, nor any ornament to be seen whatever. Her figure, at a short distance, might not ineptly be compared to a milestone with a carter's hat resting on its summit. Her once little feet are now covered with list shoes to defend them from attacks of a desultory gout which she has suffered long in both extremities. Her face, at the time I allude to, was swollen with this disorder to distortion. She has no colour, *le couleur de rose a disparu* [sic] and in its place appears a kind of dingy lilac which spreads all over her once light countenance and appears burnt into her lips. The crows-feet are wide-spreading beneath her eyes, which, though sunken, still gleam with faded lustre through her long dark eyelashes. She bears the remains of what was once superlatively lovely — the wreck of the angel's visage is yet to be seen; it looks interesting in decay — not the decay brought by age and infirmity [such as even she, Julia Johnstone must suffer, she implies], but beauty hurried away prematurely, from the practices of a licentious and dissolute life; such is the once celebrated Miss Dubochet, alias Wilson.' Julia states that she repudiates, at the urgent request of her friends, 'the vile aspersions cast on me by one who was indebted to me not only for pecuniary services, but introducing her to fashionable life …'

She is plainly mortified at the financial success of Harriette's *Memoirs*, and hopes to do as well herself. Julia, in her own words, had 'no editor like Stockdale, to wrap up in equivocal language the most sensual tales and clothe *vice* in the raiment of *virtue* ...' After a torrent of scandalous tattle she ends on a high-flown note. Her whole effort has been to repair the injury done to others by Harriette's *Memoirs*. 'Reader, I say with St. Paul, I have fought the good fight. I have finished my course, and now I care not what men can say against me.' Alas, no one bothered to say anything, for or against. The *Confessions* were a failure. She had, we suspect, been a bore in her youth and she did not change with age.

Although the manner in which Julia is described by Harriette is sometimes irritating, it is not wantonly vicious, as are all Julia's disclosures on Harriette. In the index to one edition of the *Memoirs*, Julia is listed as *Julia Storer, a girl at Hampton Court, ruined on the staircase of.* A bald statement, but it appears to have been true. She was brought up in genteel poverty, her mother being, she says, a maid of honour to Queen Charlotte. The pay was trifling and Julia often wore royal cast-offs. When the court moved to Hampton Court Palace, Julia, at fourteen, found the etiquette of the elderly Queen's court oppressive. 'One day I was handed out of the carriage by a military officer. The sight inspired me with unusual pleasure: a hussar's cap and feather gives such a fillip to the spirits of a young miss in her teens, you don't know.' She was now thrown into the society of Colonel Cotton, dashing husband of an austere lady to whose children Julia acted in the capacity of governess-companion. Soon there followed the seduction on the staircase. Inflamed with passion, the lovers threw discretion to the winds. 'When I discovered myself to be in a peculiar situation,' says Julia, 'the Colonel removed me to a cottage near Primrose Hill, where I had all the conveniences and comforts of life ...' (And five children, says Harriette.)

It was in this modest abode, about the year 1802, that Harriette first encountered Julia, who now passed as Mrs.

Johnstone, the Colonel being known as Mr. Johnstone. Harriette, then a beginner at the game, had only recently exchanged Lord Craven, 'a dead bore,' for the Honourable Fred Lamb, not much better, who had installed her in Somers Town, an easy walk from Primrose Hill. The ladies fell into conversation and, while each knew nothing of the other's circumstances, like calls to like, and a friendship was struck. 'When Lamb left Harriette alone, which was four out o f six nights,' says Julia, 'she came to me, danced or romped with the children; she was all animal spirits. I believe nothing could have made her grieve for an hour but the loss of her beauty.' One Sunday the two ladies were alone. 'Fred Lamb always dined at home that day, like a good boy.' 'Mr. Johnstone' was also absent. The ladies were soon exchanging confidences. 'We had no music and were rather dull.' But not for long.

"Come, Julia," said Harriette, "I will dispel this *ennui* by telling you my history." She started counting up her lovers which, according to Julia, was a most shocking admission. Julia's retrospectively sanctimonious tone does not ring true. She goes on to say that Harriette's family lived in a nook at Hammersmith, burrowed together like rabbits. (No mention here of the Dubochets' house which, however modest, was still in Mayfair.) Harriette's first love was, according to Julia, not Lord Craven, but the son of a washerwoman who kept a ferry-boat on the Thames below Hammersmith, where he plied for hire. 'A lusty, carroty lad, with the finest set of … teeth I ever saw': thus Harriette, according to Julia, who goes on to say that Harriette and Amy often took trips to Isleworth and back to visit another humble lover, this time Amy's, a miller, locally celebrated for his amorous prowess. For all one summer, the river idyll continued, the sisters drifting up the pale, misty reaches of the Thames, past Chiswick Mall and Strand-on-the-

Green, (much as remains today), on past the willow-fringed islands and the little Dutch palace at Kew, to the silent reaches of Sion, where the herons fly at evening and the bells of Isleworth church sound faintly across the water meadows. So they drifted, Harriette clasped to her wherry-boy, Amy in the arms of her miller. Such was the modest beginning of two such high-steppers. If we are to believe Julia, this was their true embarkation for Cytherea.

Julia says she was greatly astonished at Harriette's disclosures. "'Can this be true?'" interrupted I. "True as eggs is eggs," cried Harriette, and continued, "Then I fell sick for a recruiting sergeant who beat such tattoo on my heart he fairly turned it topsy-turvy.'" The young Harriette eloped with him, we learn, but he made off with her best clothes and her watch. 'This cooled her for low life, and she resolved to look higher says Julia, obviously satisfied to have denied the more stylish version with which Harriette opens her own tale. Since Julia Johnstone's *Confessions* are little known, and hard to come by, these extracts are of particular interest in our reconstruction of Harriette herself. And they give us a delicious picture of Miss Wilson preparing for bed. 'Harriette was a perfect nightmare in the same room with you, taking as much pains in doing up her fine hair and folding her laced night-gown and cap though she were preparing for a ballroom. I remonstrated with her once, on the folly of spending two hours thus, and then waking me out of my sleep to give my opinion on how her night-clothes became her, whether she looked most like Cleopatra waiting for Anthony, or the wife of Potiphar trying to seduce Joseph. Harriette said she would not for the world go to bed otherwise than elegant, for fear of dying in the night and not making an elegant corpse.'

However much they may have bickered in private, the Three

Graces presented a united front to the world. Besides sharing one another's boxes at the opera, they moved in and out of one another's houses, exchanged hats, lovers, good advice and confidences and put their heads together to invent all manner of elaborate ruses to catch this man or that, Harriette taking a specially sympathetic interest in 'poor Julia's' inability to retain the affections of Sir Harry Mildmay, 'the violet-breathing baronet,' as Julia described him.

All Three Graces were concerned over Sophia's precocious entry into the world of gallantry. "'*She is off!* Sophia is off! Run away, nobody knows where," was the cry of all my sisters one fine morning,' says Harriette, and goes on to recount a curious instance of the law at that time. Sophia was thirteen and had gone to Lord Deerhurst, who seduced her and then, alarmed at the protestations made by Harriette, returned Miss Sophia to her family. When they threatened to sue him, claiming he must provide for her, it was found that 'the only legal grounds for obtaining provision for a girl thus unfortunately situated is that of the parents having lost her domestic services.' Deerhurst being at last prevailed upon to provide for Sophia, his parsimony was made apparent by his choice of 'two small dark parlours near Grosvenor Place,' but to make amends, he sent her six bottles of redcurrant wine, declaring it to be far more conducive to health than any 'foreign vintage'. He further provided her with the most trumpery bits of brass and glass jewellery, which he cunningly presented in boxes bearing the label of the best jeweller's in town. Sophia's elder sisters were particularly incensed at this cruel deception, and all of them were delighted to plead Lord Berwick's cause when he wished to remove Sophia from such a stingy lover and make her his own.

Julia, however, is warm in her defence of Lord Deerhurst.

'His lordship took lodging for her near Hyde Park Corner, but it was so far from being the mean one Harriette describes that it was a first floor *in every way* becoming to the mistress of a Peer.' Sophia, she sums up as 'a pert and forward child. Harriette foolishly, if not wickedly, cockered-up her ideas with hopes of making conquests — of bringing this lord or that knight to her feet. In a very short time the little creature talked of nothing else but *leveling* a peer, *winging* a duke, *dropping* a baronet; even *hamstringing* an alderman — a vocabulary culled from the sporting peers who were Harriette's admirers.'

Sophia appears to have been so determined on her fall that we conclude she was influenced in early life by the example of a young lady called Rachel Lee, the story of whose rape by two gentlemen, (one of them in holy orders), occupied a great deal of space in the press during the year 1804. Cross-examined during the trial of these men, Rachel Lee had admitted that, when forced into the post-chaise, she found further resistance useless and, tearing from her breast a camphor bag, (evidently powerless against assault, whatever it might promise against moths), she flung it from the window and exclaimed, "The charm that has hitherto served my virtue is dissolved! Now welcome pleasure!" This admission proved fatal to the prosecution, and the accused gentlemen were given their liberty amid loud cheers from the assembled public. *Now welcome pleasure!* How often the Dubochet sisters echoed this! It was, indeed, their lifelong maxim, their guiding principle.

The Three Graces always drove together in the park on fine afternoons. It was a ritualistic outing, as much a part of their professional life as nightly appearance at the opera. Here the fair Cyprians, in their splendid equipage, circled under the trees, escorted by a cavalcade of trotting beaux. Their carriages were usually upholstered in a colour calculated cast the most becoming glow upon the occupant. Sky-blue satin was to set off a milky complexion best; ruby velvet was a glowing foil for a brunette. Fine horses, footmen and coachmen were *de rigeur*. 'The servants' hats are spiked with a cockade to imply their mistresses have seen service,' says a contemporary observer, the English Spy who gives us much information on the Fashionable Impures. He tells us he was walking in the park towards Cumberland Gate with his friends. Eglantine, Blackmantle and Crony, when they were passed by several fine equipages containing the demi-reps, out for an airing. 'In London,' he observes, 'daughters of pleasure are like physicians, travelling about to destroy in all sorts of ways.' He goes on to say that the demi-reps had the discretion leave heraldic emblazonment alone, (though one flaunted a crest; it was serpent coiled and prepared to strike). Coronets and escutcheons were wages of virtue, and poor company many of the neglected wives found them. The Duchess of Wellington, loaded with the honours of her husband's glory, was often to be seen driving alone, buried in a book; she was so shortsighted she could not recognize a face, and so shy she could never greet anyone.

A constant thread of financial worry runs through Harriette's *Memoirs* and from time to time, (as when Julia's furniture was seized by the bailiffs) there are acute crises. Still, the ladies seem to have lived in considerable style. It was every courtesan's dream to have 'money in the Funds,' the mere phrase conjuring up the most relaxing vistas of security. The Count, later Duke, of Palmella, then Portuguese Ambassador to the Court of St. James's, was so struck by Amy's swarthy charms that he won her away from a visiting Russian, Count Benckendorff, and set her up handsomely in Curzon Street, with '£200 a month paid in advance and the use of carriage'. Such were the terms. We wonder how the Countess viewed this last concession. According to Julia, Harriette squandered her money on gewgaws, and sometimes settled the jeweller's bill by payment in kind. She tells of an occasion when she accompanied Harriette to plead with old Courtois, the hairdresser and *débauché*, who threatened to sue for the £100 he had lent her. He had, besides, provided her with £800 worth of jewels, says Julia, (although Harriette always says she disdained jewels, save ear-rings, preferring to have the distinction of a simple, elegant toilette unadorned by ornament). Harriette and Courtois retired to an inner room, says Julia, who waited in the antechamber. After half an hour the old miser returned, all smiles; he kissed Harriette's hand, calling her very kind — very pretty, very kind. And no more was heard of the debt.

Harriette's extravagances, says Julia, were a drain even on Mr. Meyler, the wealthy sugar baker. 'He long afterwards felt the effects of his profusion. Her establishment in Lisson Grove was kept up in great style ... servants, equipages ... as well as his own house in Grosvenor Square.' But this was towards the end of Harriette's career. At first she seems to have been able to obtain money all around, even from those who were not technically her lovers. Prince Esterhazy, who had economical notions about love and sought diversions among the cut-rate girls of Cranborne Alley, had the effrontery to offer Harriette a ten-pound note on suggesting she should play pander for him. "There are many girls who are determined on their own fall," he said. "All I want is that when you should see them going downhill, you should give them a gentle push." Harriette was outraged, refused to oblige the Prince and read him a stiff lecture on the spot. But she pocketed the note all the same.

Gewgaws apart, she seems to have lived expensively. There are constant references to her footman, (the lugubrious Will

Halliday), her cook, the lady's maid, the housekeeper, coachman and her *dame-de-compagnie*, whose exact function is not clear. She does not seem to have entertained as much as Amy and Fanny, though no doubt, since she was such excellent company, she was in great demand, and she very often refers to supper parties at Lord Hertford's and elsewhere. Such women were always expected to live stylishly and to have, besides a good address, an elegantly furnished house, first-rate food and a well-stocked cellar.

Then there were the lesser but necessary expenses on which so much depended — the art of the stay-maker, the hairdresser and the shoemaker. Small beautifully-shaped feet were Harriette's special pride, and she spent considerable sums on her shoes. Then, too, although when under steady protection, mantua-makers' and milliners' bills were generally met by the current protector; when the Cyprians lived more freely there were stretches of time when they had no one to rely on for any steady income. Harriette was always very selective. She never suffered middle-class men willingly; it had to be aristocrats or 'the lower orders'.

When the Prince Regent moved to Brighton and established himself in his fabulous Hindu-Gothic Pavilion, the Court followed, the crack regiments were quartered there, the *beau monde* flocked and it suddenly came imperative for Harriette and her kind to be there too. Some set off in a spirit of adventure, of chase; others, such as Sophia, more fortunate, were invited there on very special terms. She had at last been persuaded to inhabit the same house as the besotted Lord Berwick, but she had not yet decided whether she could tolerate him on closer terms. This hypocritical young creature determined, even now, not to appear compromised. She insisted that her protector go ahead in a coach-and-four, followed by his servants, a *batterie de cuisine* and the silver. Miss Sophia came last, in a neat little chariot, accompanied by Julia, because, says Harriette, 'Mademoiselle Sophie wished to parade the remains of her rather shaky virtue.'

Harriette was installed at Brighton under Lord Worcester's protection some time during the year 1811. The young lover was in a fever. He had taken a house, engaged servants, ordered meals and, fiercely impatient, galloped fifteen miles along the Brighton Road to meet his mistress. Harriette was overwhelmed with his passions and attentions, he presented her with a richly embroidered side-saddle, which he said should be kept in his dressing-room, unsullied by any groom's hand. Harriette was especially touched. The accounts of their *ménage* at Rockcliffe Gardens are among her most entertaining pages.

According to Julia, a *rational* tone prevailed in the Worcester-Wilson *ménage* ... 'Domestic calmness shed its blessings ... at one time I thought Harriette stood a good chance, so firmly had she drawn the leading strings around Worcester. He was, of all the men I ever knew, the most partial to fireside comforts and rational society.'

At that moment Brighton presented a curious spectacle. The fishing village had been transformed overnight into the setting for extravagance of fashionable life, from the fabulous onion domes, pagodas and turrets of the Royal Pavilion, to the eccentricities of costume and behavior adopted by the *ton*; the in-crowd. The Court, the *beau monde*, the officers and their fancy ladies were all lodged in the little black-pebble or bow-fronted houses along the various Marine Parades, Terraces and Gardens that faced the sparkling, pale-blue expanse of the sea. The narrow lanes and winding streets were hugger-mugger with the splendour of newly imposed classic porticoes and those houses built around the Pavilion for the Prince Regent's immediate entourage. Mrs. Fitzherbert, who never inhabited the Pavilion, was ensconced in a commodious, balconied villa adjacent to, and allegedly connected with it, by an underground passage. Later this house was taken over by the Young Men's Christian Association.

The tracing of living links with other ages, with what appears the remote past, is a peculiarly fascinating study. In some cases the Restoration, and even the Tudor age, has been reached by three or four lives. The present writer remembers an old resident of Brighton who had known Mrs. Fitzherbert. Creevey mentions a certain 'young giant Spencer,' a child of the Bessborough circle, and this boy, as Sir Spencer Ponsonby Fane, was living, perfectly sound in memory, until 1915. Harriette's sister Sophia died only in 1875. That Lord Ebrington, who had been so assiduous in his attentions to Harriette in Paris, was survived by his widow till 1896, within four years of the last century; while Fred Lamb's widow lived till 1894. Perhaps the two old ladies were friends and sat together over the teacups, their veined, bony, heavily ringed hands rattling among the silver and, their footmen and companions withdrawn to a discreet distance, they spoke of the past, the trouble with husbands and the particular troubles brought about by the *Memoirs* of that forgotten temptress who had been so outspoken about poor dear Fred and Hugh.

At Regency Brighton, the sportsmen, led by Jockey Norfolk — The Duke — bet heavily on the races and spent their days between the Downs and the stables. From the banqueting rooms of the Pavilion, (where gilded dragons twined, and every Oriental conceit was incorporated in the decoration), came exotic wafts of high living, pâtés and curries, soufflés and such, mingling with the scent of the fresh currant buns baked by the pastry cooks of East Street. It was at once innocent and raffish, and the Three Graces installed there continued the sophisticated tenor of their London life — lovers and tattle, high passions and intrigue, besides bun-eating and donkey-rides along the beach.

Harriette was no stranger to Brighton. She had lived in a house on the Steine with Lord Craven, (the dead bore), in her earliest days. It was at Brighton too, that she had made her overtures to the Prince of Wales. The manner in which she was established there by Lord Worcester shows us how these ladies were accepted by the men of *ton*, by the regimental commanders too. Harriette rides with the officers, her riding habit being an exact copy of the 10th Hussars uniform. She dines in their mess, (the only woman present), and dinner is kept back an hour to suit her. She promises the Colonel personally to be responsible for Lord Worcester being on parade at 8 a.m., just as she had no doubt been responsible for his failing to be there on time so many other mornings. Harriette, more than the rest of the Cyprians, seems to have queened it over the army. It will be recalled she always had a weakness for the military of all ranks. Indeed, Julia tells us she was once ordered off the parade ground by General Hill, 'since her flirting was so insufferably indelicate that she occupied the attention of the entire regiment.'

Edmond de Goncourt observes that there is a natural partnership between the soldier and the prostitute. 'Woman's love of force, her attraction towards brutality are even more marked among such women. The soldier may be coarse, but he is neither sarcastic nor vicious, as are so many *petits bourgeois*. The prostitute feels herself the soldier's equal — his mistress — while with the other men she is simply an instrument of pleasure. But the soldier, with his hard life of discipline and danger, remains simpler. His passions are more direct. He spends his money on her generously and parades her proudly. There is no condescension.'

Perhaps this reasoning affected Harriette subconsciously. In any case she, her sisters and friends always showed a marked liking for military men — Julia for Colonel Cotton, Fanny for Colonel Parker, Amy for General Madden — and Harriette, while snubbing Wellington, seemed more partial to the Marquis of Worcester once he had donned his regimentals.

While the likenesses of many of the men who formed Harriette's immediate circle are left to us in family portraits, or caricatures, such as the well-known series by Dighton, Harriette and her sisters are less well served. Of beautiful Fanny, with her laughing dark-blue eyes, I can find no trace. Lord Hertford, connoisseur of both art and women, wished to have her painted by Sir Thomas Lawrence, but this was never done. In the crude engravings of the period Sophia, Amy, Harriette and Julia all appear plain. Sophia is downright hideous. Harriette's looks must have depended largely on her vivacity. 'She possessed a considerable portion of humour,' we learn, 'and could perform "High life below stairs" *au merveille*.' Sir Walter Scott found her ugly — men sought her more for her wit, he said. Although even Julia speaks of her once superlative loveliness, I fancy she was never, in the strict sense, a beauty. We know that she had a lovely figure, bright hazel eyes fringed with dark lashes; that she wore her brown hair dressed in loose curls; that her feet and ankles were particularly well formed; that she seldom wore colours, preferring to appear in the evening in 'a rich white figured French gauze'; that her only ornaments were long ear-rings, ruby, turquoise, or pearl. She seems to have dressed with a restrained elegance, at once *à la mode* and in her own style.

She had her own, highly personal manner of speaking, too. In a letter to Byron she speaks of herself as 'never being one to think of forms much.' Her turn of phrase, her slang, are lively. She is 'struck all of a heap' when the Beauforts withhold her allowance. According to Julia Johnstone, her oaths were startling. Sir Joseph Nourse, said Julia, held that 'Harriette would have made an excellent sailor's wife, she swore such good round oaths ... She thought it gave zest to her conversation as olives do to wine ...' Thus Julia, all prunes and prisms, and we catch a sudden flash of another Harriette, the *gamine*, who to some of her lovers was 'Harry' and to others 'little fellow' — a saucy boy rather than a passionate woman. 'No one likes me a *little*, or forgets me, when they have once liked,' she writes to Edward Bulwer-Lytton, the young novelist, in a revealing letter. [1]

Although she often speaks of fevers, coughs and ill-health, she was in fact remarkably wiry. Not for her the swooning style of *La Dame aux Camélias*. She lived hard, rode hard and walked hard too. She was, in modem parlance, athletic. She loved to walk and, before making a rendez-vous with a new lover, thought nothing of trying out his paces from Hyde Park up to Primrose Hill and down again, a walk of some eight miles or more and one which she accomplished without turning a hair, (this after nights which left little time for repose), but which on one occasion left the gentleman in question, Lord Granville Leveson-Gower, in a sweat of exhaustion. While he mopped his brow on Harriette's doorstep in Grosvenor Street and begged to be allowed to enter to recover himself, she decided he would not suit and packed him off. Found wanting on the walk, he was given no chance to justify himself otherwise.

Harriette was ever high-handed. Prospective clients who called without being correctly introduced were given short shrift. Occasionally she unbent sufficiently to say a fifty-pound note would

---

[1] The letter is quoted in full in the Appendix.

do as well as a regular introduction — fifty pounds being, at that time, a very large sum. Once a peer of the realm made so bold as to send his footman with a note soliciting the honour of a rendez-vous that night. This business-like request flung Harriette into a rage. She pealed her bell, (one of her favourite gestures), and ordered the footman out, but not before she had returned his master's letter to him — unsealed, unfolded, for all the world to read — saying, 'This letter could not be meant for me, to whom he only presented yesterday. Take it back, young man, and say from me that I request he will be careful how he misdirects them in future — an accident which was no doubt caused by his writing them after dinner'. We imagine with what pleasure the footman must have loitered on the way back, recounting it all among the shopkeepers, stable boys and publicans of Mayfair.

On the other hand, Harriette herself often made overtures to gentlemen she fancied, or whose money she coveted, and she was always very much put out if they did not respond favourably. But on the whole she had few rebuffs and seems not only to have enjoyed the exercise of her calling, but to have been able to pick and choose among the quality. We have it on her own authority that she sometimes suffered from *le diable au corps* and allowed herself to be carried away by an enthusiasm fatal to her profession. She found Mr. Meyler, 'the damned sugar baker,' as Lord Alvanley called him, perfectly irresistible. 'There was in fact an expression in Meyler's countenance of such voluptuous beauty that it was impossible for any woman to converse with him, after he had dined, in cold blood'. Harriette, decidedly warm-blooded, led him a dance equalled only by that which he led her. She took an understandable pleasure, too, in taking him away from the Duchess of Beaufort, Lord Worcester's mother, who had been so unsympathetic to Harriette's affair with her son.

Although Harriette had such a weakness for the military, she shows also a particular liking for gentlemen of a more intellectual kind. Lord Ponsonby was not a Corinthian; he was considerably older than she and of a more studious cast than most of his contemporaries. In fact, to be worthy of his love, Harriette shut herself up and read Seneca. 'The Greeks employed me for two whole days,' she says, 'and the Romans six more ... I then read Rousseau's *Confessions*, then Racine's Tragedies and, afterwards, Boswell's *Life of Johnson*. I allowed myself only ten minutes for my dinner,' adds this ardent creature who never did anything by halves. Julia speaks of Harriette having literary aspirations, and it is certain that she revered Byron the poet beyond the fashionable cult of Lord Byron as the rage and scandal of the town. ('I always should have been more proud of the slightest acquaintance with you than being loved dearly as I was by Wellington and other great men in my time,' she writes.) In her attitude towards him she shows an almost maternal solicitude. It is, perhaps, only in her letters to Lord Byron that we can gauge Harriette's nature fully. In these letters we see something more than the 'smart, saucy girl' Sir Walter Scott remembered. In the *Memoirs* she quotes some remarkably dull letters which she says are among those she sent to Byron. Evidently she did not keep copies and had forgotten all but their purport. A century later a small packet of her letters to the poet was discovered among the Byron papers in the possession of Sir John Murray, whose great-grandfather had been the poet's publisher and confidant.

These letters give us the living, warm, witty Harriette as she was when no considerations of her calling came between her and the object of her affection. [2] Harriette emerges from the

---

[2] Two of those letters are quoted in full in the Appendix.

spidery scrawl as a woman full of common sense, humour, tenderness too, which her conduct regarding the *Memoirs* might lead us to suppose she had long lost. Besides the letters to Lord Byron there are three which she addressed ten years or so later, probably in 1829, to the novelist Edward Bulwer-Lytton. Here we see, once again, the forgotten demi-rep at forty-three, still longing, if not for conquests, for some link with that world of gaiety, literature and politics in which she had once lived. These letters are less emotional than those to Lord Byron, but they give as Harriette's lively self and show conclusively her own style — the style of the *Memoirs*, thus proving that these were not, as is sometimes said, the work of either Stockdale, or some unknown hack.

Here is Harriette writing to Byron. The letter is undated, but probably can be set around 1818. 'I love you honestly and dearly ... *Your* love I never desired ... Pray, dear Lord Byron, think of me a little, now and then, (I don't mean as a woman for I shall never be a *woman* to you) ... forget me when you are happy; but in gloomy moments, chilly, miserable weather, bad razors and cold water, perhaps you'll recollect and write to me.' 'Miserable weather, bad razors and cold water.' How succinctly she sums up those moments of *cafard*, moments when love means little and friendship alone can cheer. There are a number of such solicitous letters. True, she importuned for money, (which Byron sometimes sent), but always, to him, she offered warmth and tenderness. 'I wish I could learn something of your *health*, dear Lord Byron.' In another, chiding him for some splenetic outburst, some passage she considers unworthy of his genius, occasioned, she suspects, by liver: 'Throw away your pen, my love, and take a little calomel,' she urges. And if he replied, the letters have vanished, along with other traces of Harriette Wilson's life, her possessions, or souvenirs.

There is a legend, which I am unable to trace, that somewhere in the green, quiet landscape of northern England a house still stands richly furnished, but unoccupied, since Harriette refused it. One of her more generous admirers had hoped to lure her to the country and his embraces by preparing this gilded cage. But Harriette, 'never one for ruralizing,' would have none of it. The house has stood empty ever since. By the terms of the owner's Will, it may not be sold, let, or in any way changed.

Of Harriette's taste in houses and furniture we know nothing. Egyptian and Gothic extravaganzas were now the rage in many of the stately homes. Remodelled dining-rooms became echoing vaults; there were monastic corridors and vast cathedral bedrooms with pinnacled, fretted tomb-like beds and dressing-tables resembling high altars. It is in such setting that we imagine the sinister witch-women that Fuseli's drawings represent, all evil in their beckoning glance. They are the fitting denizens of such a horrific setting. Impudent and robust Harriette has no place here. Creevey writing of Knowsley, when the new Gothic dining-room was opened, and describing it as being fifty-three by thirty-seven feet and 'such a height that it destroys the effect of all the other apartments ... You enter it from a passage, by two great Gothic church-like doors the whole height of the room.' (It will be recalled that when Beckford built Fonthill Abbey — where the arches of the great hall were one-third higher than the loftiest arches of the nave in Westminster Abbey — he stationed a dwarf at the doors to emphasize their height.) Creevey goes on, 'General Grosvenor was heard to remark, "Pray are those great doors to be opened for every pat of butter that comes into the room?"' In spite of two fireplaces, thirty-six wax candles and ten great pedestal lamps, the cold was still quite petrifying and Creevey says they were soon obliged to abandon the room entirely.

And now the mood changes, the skies cloud over and the villain appears. Harriette had known high comedy, drama, and a certain pathos too. But not until she encountered the sinister figure of William Henry Rochfort did her way lead irrevocably into the shadows. The swaggering creature who now appears was to become the baleful influence of her life. Up to this time Harriette's path, however thorny, had been lit by the brightness of youth and health and hope, a morning glow, where adventures, loves and griefs, however desperate, were all part of the pattern of a demi-rep's life, unshadowed by what was to follow. Even the spectre age, advancing so implacably, had been foreseen and accepted as something inevitable, as she herself said in a letter to Byron:

> *'I will hope that we shall one day, some twenty years hence, take a pinch of snuff together before we die — and as you watch me in my little pointed cap, spectacles, bony ankles and thread stockings, stirring up and tasting my pot-au-feu, you'll imagine Ponsonby's, Worcester's and Argyle's Angelick Harriette.'*

With this melancholy but classic end in view, Harriette had withdrawn to Paris, where she was declining by stages, from a *rechauffée* of rather indifferent ex-lovers and second-rate, come-by-chance protectors to boys such as the very young Secretary of Embassy whom, in another letter to Byron, she tells us she set to searching out her grey hairs.

Old ways die hard. The habits of coquetry and badinage, the thirst for admiration and power over men, the craving for the stimulus of adventure were ingrained and, like her lusty appetites, her passions and frailties had been fostered by the example of her giddy elder sisters. Those habits, begun so young, had become the inclinations and necessities, the very mainspring, of a lifetime. How could she change her whole nature? As long as there were men to fool, to flirt with and, who knows, perhaps still to love, the game of hearts must continue.

But boys, even those enamoured young scions of nobility, who had been reared on whispered legends of Harriette's glory, could be no more than puppet partners in a twilight epilogue. Decidedly it did not do to play the game of hearts in Paris.

Some time between the years 1815-1820, she returned to London, drawn there perhaps by a nostalgia for the scenes of her former triumphs, by loneliness, by family ties and the fading hopes of encountering some long-lost love — of catching a glimpse of Ponsonby, even. Who knows what secret longings, what romantic hopes she cherished beneath what was becoming a rather battered, but still brave exterior? That Harriette was capable of loving deeply, of suffering, there is no doubt. Anguish sounds occasionally through her flippancies. In yet another letter to Lord Byron, written, it would seem, about this time, we see the real woman, all barriers down. It is a tragic cry, wrung from the heart:

> *'Lord, if only you could suffer for a single day the agony of mind I endured for more than two years after Ponsonby left me, because Mrs. Fanny [Lord Ponsonby's wife] would have it so, you would bless your stars and your good fortune, blind, deaf and lame at eighty-two, so that you could sleep an hour in forgetfulness, eat a little bit of batter pudding. Heavens! How I have prayed for death, nights, days and months together, merely as a rest from suffering ...'*

Unhappily there was never any rest for Harriette; she was a
constant prey to both her emotions and her appetites. Now,
once more, her heart was to be wrung, this time for a far less
worthy subject than Lord Ponsonby. The scene is London; the
occasion one of her rare visits, when we imagine her wandering
forlornly through the settings of her heyday, wandering like a
revenant down St. James's where 'the rattle and dash of the dice-
box' still sounded or, turning northward, catching faint echoes
of the laughter, the sound of corks being drawn, the gaiety and
chatter as it drifted out on the night air from the little house in
York Place where she and Amy and Fanny and Julia had once
held court; catching, perhaps, the echo of a door slamming shut
— Lord Ponsonby's door in Upper Brook Street, shutting her
out forever from his life.

On one of these sad evenings, as she walked home to her
lodgings in Lisson Grove, near to that establishment she had
once shared with the voluptuous Mr. Meyler, a dark shadow fell
across her path and she met her destiny in the person of
Rochfort. It was a pick-up, a street acquaintanceship, struck as
the flash bully and the fading charmer came face to face under
the flickering gas-lamps of Marylebone. For Harriette it was a
lightning dart of passion; a violent, pent-up force of emotion
was now loosed, sweeping her along. Rochfort was a prince
among men! Apollo, Mars, the King of Hearts! We imagine this
swarthy, swaggering individual who worked such havoc, whose
insolent glance was so seducing, and the haggard, eager woman
Harriette had become, levelling the full battery of her practised
arts only to be met with a contemptuous offhand acquiescence.
We do not know what Rochfort thought of Harriette; certainly
he did not return her affections wholeheartedly. To him she was
probably just one more of a string of easy conquests — one who
was to show great devotion, however, and whose energy and

dispatch in attending to his welfare made her worth cultivating. Also one who, as he came to know her better, offered all kinds of interesting possibilities of financial returns which he was, in due course, to exploit to the full.

William Henry Rochfort is a mysterious character. He appears suddenly on the scene and, having played out his part, disappears as abruptly. He claimed to be the rightful heir to an Irish earldom which had become extinct in 1814. When pressed for details, however, he always became very vague. His claims centred around the probable indiscretion of the wife of the first Earl of Rochfort. William Henry held that he was the child of a son of Lady Rochfort's by an unknown lover. Lord Rochfort refused to acknowledge this son. On the death, without issue, of the rightful heir, William Henry Rochfort claimed that the titles and estates in Ireland were his by rights. In any case, however plausible women — and Harriette in particular — found him, the law was less sympathetic, and he never succeeded in establishing his claims. In fact, on one occasion he ran foul of the law and was indicted on a charge of larceny. Julia Johnstone tells us that he had been 'for a very short time a Colonel in some unknown corps of South American Independents, and a full Cornet in Lincoln Stanhope's regiment, the 17th Dragoons, and has never clipped his moustachioes since' — a heavy sarcasm this, for the rank of cornet was very small fry, lowliest of all the officers, corresponding to a junior second lieutenant. There are few contemporary sources, reliable or otherwise, from which anything can be gleaned about the Colonel. Even his place in Lincoln Stanhope's Central American Independents remains obscure.

At this time Central and South America exercised a powerful spell over the imaginations of Europeans. This part of the world had only lately appeared on their horizons — a remote, exotic panorama. It is probable that Rochfort took full advantage of a background at once so rare and so much in vogue. No doubt he realized that such a setting added great lustre to any adventures which he recounted to Harriette, or any of the other impressionable ladies to whom he was addicted. No doubt they saw him striding fearlessly across cactus-studded deserts, swimming crocodile-infested yellow rivers which wound through tropical jungles where swarms of butterflies darkened the blazing noonday sun. They saw him, Simón Bolívar's peer, riding a plunging mustang towards liberation, his sword flourished aloft.

Did they perhaps see him as one of the few survivors, one of the guard which had accompanied that band of gullible fools, two hundred or more, victims of 'The Poyais Hoax', who, about this time, had been persuaded to pay fancy prices to the 'agents' of some promised faraway land in Central America where they were to take up the high offices and positions they had bought so trustingly in London? The celebrated hoax had appeared so convincing that, led on by accounts of streets paved with silver and hills veined with gold, of pomegranates and plenty, the two hundred citizens had embarked trustingly, accompanied by their families, servants and a troop of mercenaries.

Their true situation was revealed to them only when the ships put in to a barren stretch of coast where nothing stirred, where no sign of life was to be seen. They had been duped, they realized, and now they were to be dumped, left to perish. Hostile natives and fever decimated their ranks. Soon almost all of them were dead. Only a handful of survivors managed to return to tell the tale. It would be a dramatic episode in Rochfort's life, a properly flamboyant background for his villainy, but unfortunately there is absolutely no evidence that supports the supposition, beyond the fact that he had seen service with some

Central American Independents. In London, he soon so worked on Harriette's feelings that she was in a pining state. She learned that he was a prisoner within the Rules — the confines set for the inmates of the Debtors' Prison, confines which still left considerable freedom to move about. Before long she had paid his debts and liberated him, perhaps on the understanding that they should go through a form of marriage, and they left England together to take up their residence in Paris, Harriette now passing as Mrs. Rochfort. We imagine with what naïve delight she saw herself setting out on a last shining, eternal love — a love that was to be her all, the redemption of former ways. She would love the Colonel as she had never loved before, his every wish her law. Now that his debts were paid, now that she had detached him from the various ladies who had surrounded him so jealously in London, Harriette must have felt he was indeed all hers to cosset.

It is sentimental and probably misguided to see Harriette as a pathetic figure. But while never approaching tragic stature and being far to gallant, too much of a fighter, too little of a sniveller to be 'in the pathetics', (her own phrase), for long, she is often touched with melancholy. When we observe her more closely, weighing up her outrageous conduct and the circumstances of her life, giving her the sober consideration she is seldom accorded, she emerges as something far less dimensional than a first estimate presupposes. Compare her to another even higher flying courtesan who cloaked her activities under political intrigues, a *mari complaisant* and an Imperial lover — the Contessa di Castiglione. She was the pawn of Cavour, the Italian statesman: the greatest beauty and a scheming, arrogant, humourless egocentric. When beauty faded nothing was left but darkness, moanings, shrouded mirrors and shuttered windows. She became a shapeless bag of self-pity, living in the past, creeping out at night to rummage in the garbage bins. No backbone, no personality emerged when the façade crumbled.

Harriette, on the contrary, while often appalling us by her conduct, steadily gains our affections and interest. We follow patiently, with sympathy, her sentimental vacillations between the Duke of Leinster and Lord Worcester or, history repeating itself, between Lord Ebrington and Mr. Meyler. We positively respect her delicacy in disliking to be on with the new love while the old love still breathes the same air — though it might be said that such delicacy, in her profession, amounts to a disadvantage, is not businesslike, and Harriette is always the one to suffer. If only could talk a little common sense into the girl! All those longings and regrets over Lord Ponsonby are sad reading, no part of a demi-rep's make-up. As for her impetuous decision to write to Lord Worcester after undertaking, (the price of her pension), to remain aloof, it shows a most foolish fondness. But she will never learn. Her passion for Colonel Rochfort fills us with misgivings. He is a cad. But, as Shakespeare says, "'tis the strumpet's plague to beguile many, but be beguiled by one …' Harriette cannot rest till she has obtained the doubtful satisfaction of a Fleet marriage to her Colonel, 'Moustachio,' as she calls him. We could wish it otherwise. In short, she has become a matter of concern to us. She has come alive, and, with all her failings, we love her to the end.

There is a silence of some years before Harriette again emerges from the shadows. These years must have been sadly disillusioning. Harriette's looks have vanished. Rochfort leads her a terrible dance and drink is the only panacea. Life is hard now and getting harder with each passing day. The Colonel must be kept in those luxuries without which he becomes sulky and restive. What course is left open to the ruined, forgotten demi-rep Harriette has become? She is shrewd enough to know she can hold him just as long as she can provide for him well. Drink, snug quarters, money for gambling and for other women — those are the Colonel's requirements. Harriette casts about desperately for a means of raising money. Once she had been in the habit of plaguing her old friends for donations, but gradually they had proved less and less responsive. Harriette tells us that she cared little about money for herself; but Rochfort's spell changed everything. It has been said that Rochfort bore a certain resemblance to Harriette's great love. Lord Ponsonby, and in her now rather clouded mind it is likely that Rochfort came to represent all love, that he seemed the embodiment of Romance, as once Lord Ponsonby had been. The lodestar of her life had changed its outward semblance perhaps, but its essence may have remained the same, an unattainable, tormenting mirage.

Although there is no portrait of Rochfort to support the theory that he resembled Lord Ponsonby, it is very possibly true, for again and again we see men and women seeking to find once more in a new love some resemblance to the features, voice, eyes or mannerisms of the first person deeply loved. And it often happens that in so doing they blind themselves to fadings of character, or differences of birth and education in a touching effort to catch echoes of what had once meant so much to them. Women in particular have been known to follow men of dissolute or even criminal character, drunkards, bullies and murderers only because of a way of smiling, a look in the eyes, that gave them once again the illusion of lost love.

This may have been Harriette's case. To the objective reader it would explain Rochfort's hold on her. How otherwise accept that such a man, so low a type, could have such complete power over a woman like Harriette who had known, and been loved by, men of a very different order? Was she following the usual course of a prostitute's life by ending with hard-drinking bully for her mate? Did Rochfort, with his bogus rank and his pretensions to breeding, represent someone whom she could present to the world as her husband, but who in fact took the place those lusty common soldiers whom, by all accounts, Harriette had found irresistible in the past? Or did Rochfort, in one person, combine her love for Ponsonby and her taste for low life? Did he represent to her both sacred and profane love?

While Harriette is still fixed on the tormenting mirage of perfect love, the Colonel has other ideas. His is a wolfish temper. The frustrated child a bastard son, he feels himself slighted; denied. He longs for vengeance on that class which had ignored him and to which he feels he rightfully belongs. And so, by stages, he comes to the idea of working off his own scores on the aristocracy as a whole through the medium of Harriette, while at the same time putting a handsome sum of money into both pockets. Harriette can be a unique instrument of vengeance, for she knows all their secrets. She can easily enough be persuaded to fall in with any plan he presents. The Colonel knows his hold on her, knows how crack the whip. 'I am not my own mistress,' she writes to Bulwer-Lytton some years later. No doubt where the Colonel was concerned Harriette remained obedient. Again she harps on her changed ways: 'In fact, I am a true faithful wife leading about as innocent a life as a hermit can well do.'

Did Rochfort approach Stockdale and suggest the publication of *Memoirs*? It is perhaps not too much to imagine this may have been case. At any rate, once Stockdale had sounded Harriette, the die was cast. Harriette saw it in its simplest light, a way — her only remaining way — to earn the money she needed to keep Rochfort by her side. The *Memoirs* were begun and, no doubt spurred on by a suddenly transformed, affectionate Rochfort, Harriette's pen raced along the page, recalling this audacity or that. Stockdale, delighted by the first instalment, assured her of a huge sale. The Colonel hung over her tenderly; and together, in a most unwonted harmony, they discussed the future instalments.

We imagine them in some grey, panelled salon, a little room in one of those shuttered houses along the Faubourg St. Honoré where, built around an inner courtyard, the ground-floor rooms, however brightly lit by chandeliers and candles, are forever gloomy and overcast. Harriette wears an elegant if rather shabby, satin dress; her greying hair still in those careless curls which were Lord Worcester's undoing that evening at the opera when he was coquettishly invited to tumble them. She is seated at a desk overflowing with papers, journals, old household accounts, dunning letters, *billets doux* and bundles of Lord Worcester's effusions carefully tied up with pink tape, last traces of the lawyers who had conducted her case against the Duke of Beaufort. The lamplight falls on her haggard face. She glances up apprehensively at Rochfort, who stands over her. Harriette is as clay. She begins to scribble obediently, and as she writes a gleam of the old fun flashes from beneath the long dark lashes that even Julia Johnstone could not deny her. To Julia all the villainy was centred in Harriette. Rochfort was her fancy man, a mere accessory. But then Julia, 'seldom in the melting mood, especially when writing her *Confessions,* never saw Harriette other than as a monster of depravity. Her malice seems only to produce a caricature, the devil in petticoats. If Julia had really believed Harriette to be so evil, why had she been such a close friend of hers for so many years when they were both young?

No, we remain unconvinced and cast about for more logical, or psychological, explanations of Harriette's action. To the present writer the key is Rochfort and the spell he cast over his inamorata.

With the publication of the *Memoirs,* Harriette's financial worries were over — for a while, at any rate. Julia states that between them Harriette and Stockdale 'fingered £10,000 of the public's money.' But while they had shared these rich profits, Stockdale, as publisher, was presently involved in a series of lawsuits for libel and damages which, however, did not involve Harriette. The wretched man emerged from one suit only to be engulfed by another. Prison followed, on technicalities regarding other, more positively pornographic, or obscene publications, until at last he was ruined. Harriette seems to have had no remorse. Indeed it is difficult to be sympathetic towards Stockdale. He was an unctuous, creeping character, hypocritical, mean, sly, parasitic and unscrupulous, whose persecutions, as he called them, were the fruits of many years of villainy and culminated only in the business of the *Memoirs.*

And so Harriette now found herself snugly placed with the proceeds of the *Memoirs* in her bank, the Colonel at her side. She had become a best-selling author. Thirty-one editions were sold in the first year, pirated editions appeared all over Europe. Harriette next tried her hand at a novel, the story of English people on a visit to Paris. This indifferent piece of work, *Paris Lions and London Tigers,* is a *roman à clef* which, once characters are established — Sir Violet Sigh-away for Sir Harry Mildmay and such — has no further interest and is best forgotten, although one brief autobiographical flash can be detected. Harriette writes of a Mr. Bellfield, a paragon, evidently modelled on her image of the Colonel, and we hear Harriette, with all her longings, doubts and regrets, sounding through the paeans. '"Mr. Bellfield is a *fine* man," sighed the heroine, for with all her vanity, long experience had put it beyond a doubt that such first-rate beauties as Bellfield were past praying for.' And it is in the preface to this book that the following characteristic passage occurs: '"Here's a piece of pork and greens," as exclaimed a good-humoured countryman who got into some dilemma with his carthorse one day. "Here's a piece of pork and greens!"'

And a piece of pork and greens it was, every time Harriette reappeared on the English scene, or was reported to be brewing some further mischief. She had no sooner landed at Dover than she was set on by an outraged lady, (perhaps one whose husband figured in the *Memoirs*), who knocked her down and dragged out her hair in fistfuls. The *Memoirs* had succeeded in destroying the peace of mind of married women of all ranks. Although the book was, naturally, kept away from young ladies, those who were fortunate enough to lay hands on a copy found their confidence in the married state sadly shaken. On the other hand, hitherto undreamed vistas were now revealed to them of an alluring, independent life passed in the company of half the most desirable gentlemen in England. Harriette had much to answer for, and it is surprising she contrived to end her days in England, although as to how and where she died, we remain in the dark.

Her last public appearance was in 1829, when she had returned from Paris and was living in Trevor Square, still with the Colonel, her brother and a French maid, whom Harriette accused of improper relations with her brother. The maid retaliated by taking Harriette to court on a charge of assault. Harriette's reappearance in the limelight was a brief, inglorious flash. On 15 February, she was hailed before the magistrate at Marlborough Street. Harriette and the Colonel found themselves unsympathetically treated by the newspapers, which gloated over her vanished looks, the Colonel's inability to establish his ancestry, and their joint inability to raise bail. There were many persons of quality, said Harriette, who would vouch for her, but whom she hardly liked to trouble on so trivial a matter. After a lot of unpleasantness, she and the Colonel were allowed to depart.

It was from Trevor Square in 1830 that Harriette, anonymously, published another *roman à clef* called *Clara Gazul*, in which she refers to herself as 'Harriette Memoirs' and gives us, besides some account of her beginnings, further impudent anecdotes of the world in which she no longer figured. There is no explanation as to why she selected the name Prosper Merimée had chosen, in 1825, for his *Théâtre de Clara Gazul*. The book aroused considerable anxiety all around, and it is probable that she was persuaded to suppress most of the copies and disappear, conveniently, on receipt of a lump sum. In any case, examples of the book are very rare and it does not seem to have circulated widely.

She gave up the house in Trevor Square in 1830. After 1832 she vanishes from sight. The rest is rumour and conjecture. The little house, No. 16, at the south-east corner looks much as it did during her occupancy. The prim brick-and-plaster façade overlooks the gardens of the square where lilac, laurel and acacia tangle behind the iron railings. These quiet, elegant little streets and squares around Knightsbridge and the Park, are especially evocative of Regency life and loves. Trevor Square, Montpelier Terrace and Hill Street (now called Trevor Place) were all favourites of the demi-reps.

Sometimes, walking at night along these deserted

pavements, where only a few gas lamps still light the way where, behind the ornate balconies, muslin curtains filter an apricot glow of warmth and firelight plays across the ceding of an upstairs room, I fancy I catch a burst of laughter, a snatch of song and the chink of glasses as the Cyprians entertain their friends. Far away, wafted across the chimneys and tiled rooftops, comes the faint sound of a street organ, grinding out some forgotten tune. Harriette's house stands mute, telling nothing of that life it once framed. In 1975 the owners, who were unaware of its history, said they thought it was haunted. The ghost is a quiet one; it walks upstairs and goes into the bedroom — which is, after all, what might be expected of Harriette Wilson's shade.

Appendix

Letters

THE FOLLOWING two letters were probably written between 1812–20

HARRIETTE WILSON TO LORD BYRON

May 31st

I have received the 1000 francs and must repeat my very sincere thanks to you, dear Lord Byron. Though it was too had to cut me off with such a shabby short letter and such an excuse — just to choose the very moment when the Horse was waiting and the divorce going on. However, it is a very nice dear little letter, written more after my style than your own and, if you were not aware of it, so much the more flattering to me — I love the little cramped hand too now, and know every turn of it.

    Pray, dear Lord Byron, think of me a little now and then (I don't mean as a woman, for I shall never be a woman to you) merely as a good little fellow who feels a warmer interest in all that happens to you and all that annoys you than anybody else in the world. Forget me when you are happy; but in gloomy moments, chilly miserable weather, bad razors and cold water, perhaps you'll recollect and write to me. You can easily judge by a woman's scribbling whether her heart is with it, and you know I love you honestly and dearly. Alas! I can never prove it by any sacrifice …

    I am truth and nothing but the truth. I looked at you for half an hour together one night and while studying your very beautiful countenance I could fancy a new sensation produced by the pressure of your lips to mine, beyond what my nature could endure — wild and eager as your poetry — terrifying by its power to wither and destroy me.

Jupiter was all powerful in a cloud and ladies have been known to admire a Horse, hut there is a quieter, better, more voluptuous feeling for a woman, and you can't give it her.

Besides, I never loved any but blue eyes. Are you as dark as at the Masquerade, or were you painted? Nothing, I suppose, will ever bring you to Paris, not even your friend T. Moore; yet I will hope that we shall one day (some twenty years hence) take a pinch of snuff together before we die; and as you watch me, in my little pointed cap, spectacles, bony ankles and thread stockings, stirring tip and tasting my pot au feu, you'll imagine Ponsonby's,

Worcester's and Argyle's Angelick Harriette!

I have made a new conquest lately — Lord Francis Cunningham; but I hate boys so I have been setting him to hunt and pull out my grey hairs to destroy his illusions. He found ten and I did not know I had one. "Better get a Monkey," you'll say, than a fine young blue-eyed man of one and twenty. What a fool he must be! When you and I meet, I shall set you to work at the brown ones, for I mean to attack them as soon as the grey predominates. It is more dignified to keep to one colour, n'est-ce-pas? ...

I trust and hope "at this present writing" you are out of your scrape, or I shall be the more sorry because I know you did not love her enough to make the scrape worthwhile. Pray, dearest, let me love you, tell me to love you.

I am at a very harmless distance, you know ...

Votre Affectionée,
BEAU PAGE

God bless you; nobody knows anything about loving you but myself.

HARRIETTE WILSON TO LORD BYRON

*"This comes hopping" to say I have lost lots of my liking for you —
Il vaudrait bien la peine de faire payer un port de lettre pour si peu
de chose! But now you have paid it, you may as well learn all about
it, you know. Strange to tell, I never heard of Don Juan till I found
it on Galignani's table yesterday and took it to bed with me, where
I contrived to keep my large quiet good-looking brown eyes open
(now, you know, they are very handsome) till I had finished it.*

*Dear adorable Lord Byron, don't make a mere coarse old
libertine of yourself. When everybody advised you not to publish your
English Bards, you would mind nobody. I am nobody: therefore
attend to me. What harm did the Commandments (no matter by
whom composed, whether god or mortal) ever do you or anybody else,
and what catch-penny ballad writer could not make a parody on
them? When you don't feel quite up to a spirit of benevolence, the en-
couragement of which you are pretty sure contributes more to one's
earthly happiness than anything else, in gratitude for the talent
which, after all, must have caused you exquisite moments in your
time, throw away your pen, my love, and take a little calomel. I wish
the Deuce had all the papers, pens and ink burning, frizzling and
drying up in the very hottest place in his dominions, rather than you
should use them to wilfully destroy the respect and admiration of
those who deserve to love you and all the fine illusions with which
my mind was filled. Ecoutez, mon Ange. It is not in my power or my
nature to forget any kindness shown me (supposing I had not half
loved you before) but I would not, even to you, who in a wrong-
headed moment wrote it, lie under the imputation of such bad taste
as to admire what in your cool moments, I am sure, you must feel to
be vulgar at least ... In the very act of writing you felt half ashamed
of what you wrote; and so don't, dearest Lord Byron, keep "all on"
to the end of time mistaking mere false pride and temper for a bad*

heart; for you know all you have done or written that was wrong has caused you to regret, that convinced yourself alone (or rather you and I, my Angel) of the natural goodness of your disposition. Only, you are spoiled. Lord, if you could only suffer for one single day the agony of mind I endured for more than two years after Ponsonby left me, because Mrs. Fanny would have it so, you would bless your stars and your good fortune, blind, deaf and lame at eighty-two, so that you could sleep an hour in forgetfulness, or eat a little bit of batter pudding. Heavens! How I have prayed for death, nights, days, and months together, merely as rest from suffering and you! whom everybody loves or wishes to love ... Don't bore yourself to answer my nonsense. I hate people to bore themselves for me. Reading Don Juan made me think of you all day; and so I could not go to bed without presuming to write to you again. But I won't quarrel with you for not answering. Only, pray, don't say anything harsh to me ... don't forget this most flattering expression in a former letter of yours: "I now trust this most brilliant acquaintance may be permitted to end." I was more angry than hurt then, knowing myself not deficient in natural or affecting brilliancy. I thought you a coxcomb and myself a much better subject; but now if you are unkind to me I shall die of it. In the meantime, I am dying for want of sleep; so God bless you, dear Lord Byron, and

    good night.

HARRY

HARRIETTE WILSON TO E. BULWER-LYTTON

Part of a letter from Harriette Wilson to Edward Bulwer-Lytton, probably written in 1829. She was forty-three and living in Paris on her memories and the profits of her *Memoirs*, while he had become the newest, most fashionable English novelist:

Sir,

Though I have disliked reading all my life unless it be Shakespeare's plays, yet I got to the end of Pelham. It was not a book to my taste either, for I thought the writer was a cold hearted man, and his light chit chat was pedantic, smelling of the Lamp — not so good as my own. But then it was a sensible book, the fancies brilliant, the thought deep, the language very expressive. In short I got to the end of it. The Disowned I liked better still and felt very much obliged to you for writing one of the few books I can come to the end of, with all my desire for amusement. But that imbecile (Mordaunt) who allow'd his wife to be starved like a helpless blockhead, his want of French philosophy made me sick. Do you consider that man virtuous or sensible whose little soul makes him ashamed of doing his duty in that state of life into which it may please God to call him? He had arms and legs, health and intelligence — why did not he clean his wife's room and whitewash the walls, earn her by his daily work a mutton chop, and then fry it for her à la Maintenon? There's no such thing as starving in England for an intelligent man who will turn his hand to anything rather than endure to see the beloved of his soul die of hunger. No, that man ought to have been sent to the treadmill.

Now for Devereux, I have nearly finished the first vol. and am so charmed with it, that I have laid it aside to tell you how proud I should be if you felt disposed to honour me with your acquaintance. I merely suggest this to you because life is too short and too miserable for us to afford prudently to risk the loss of a possible pleasure for want of asking for it, and it is just possible that we might derive pleasure from being acquainted — not very probable, however, because I am not a bit agreeable except to those who are predisposed to like me and who appear to feel and understand all that is original, or eccentric, or amusing, or likeable in my character at once. I am very shy, and when people do not flatter and encourage me by making me feel sure of their predisposition to like me, I am not a bit amiable because I am genée. I am not, and never was, a general favourite; but nobody likes me a little, or forgets me when they have once liked, understood and been liked by me. I am very ignorant and can't spell, but there is this advantage in not reading, you are all of you copies and I am the thing itself. You are sure if I say anything to strike or please you that it came out of my own little head.

What do you think about it? Perhaps you would like my society better than I should like yours ... I am not ugly, as they describe me in the papers; but on the contrary rather handsome, particularly by candlelight when I am amused — although I was born at ten minutes before eight o'clock, the 22 February 1786 and christened at St. George's Church — I love to be particular.

I am not my own mistress, but if en tout bien et tout honneur you were to write me a word that you would not object to favour me with a visit some day — or will you take a walk with me some evening? I am much pleasanter to begin with when I am walking, because if it is dark I thus get rid of the shyness enough to be indulgent.

Yours truly, and with high respect for your superior talents,
HENRIETTE ROCHFORT
Author of The Memoirs of Harriette Wilson.

The following are some extracts from another letter written by Harriette Wilson to Edward Bulwer-Lytton in 1829, where it is evident that the elegant and cautious young man refuses to respond to Harriette's advances. That is, he encourages the flattering correspondence but refuses to compromise himself by meeting her in person. But Harriette, hungry for amusement, and for echoes of that world of clever, high-bred men which she had once known, refuses the rebuff and tries to interest him in her novel *Clara Gazul*. But he will have neither the lady nor her book, and we feel he is the loser.

October 1st, *deux heures après minuit*
(1829)

*Though my sister gave me your letter before dinner (in answer
to mine O, "the six weeks ago instant") I had no opportunity of
reading it till this moment. I am sleepy and my fire is out, and yet,
the matter having hold of my thoughts, I should not rest till I had
expressed to you my regret that you like me, since you refuse to shake
hands with me. On sait à peu près ce qu'on veut, I had therefore
philosophically made up my mind to endure your silent contempt,
but since you are benevolently inclined towards me, it is really rather
hard upon me this — dead cut. From your style of writing I did not
expect to find you a very agreeable companion for a post-chaise, etc.,
nor did I desire that we should meet under the impression that it was
at all incumbent on us to be more agreeable than our neighbours. The
very thought and fever of such a wish would only serve to redden
our noses and dampen our spirits. I conceived, as a sensible man, you
might be amused with the novelty of a woman who is always true to
nature, no matter how bizarre may be her thoughts, creed, or wishes.
However, if you won't make friends with me you won't, and I must
stick to my "Yours of the 15th came safe to hand on the, etc."*

*If, however, you believe I wished you to neglect others for so in-
significant an individual as myself, you have done me injustice.
Believing you only desired the honour of your acquaintance under
the impression that love or desire for me now I was entirely out of
the chapter of possibilities, and that no wife would pay me the
compliment to object to my occasionally enjoying the benefit of a little
chat with her husband. I should have been proud and obliged if
hereafter you would have been at the trouble of looking over my
unfinished new Work — the only thing I have ever written at all to
my own satisfaction with regard to romance, the language and the
spirit of it. But why should I have presumed to expect so much con-*

descension from you? The work must take its chance; I'll publish it with all its blunders of ignorance, because I like it myself, and expect others may do so too, since everybody tells me I had never had any vanity. What I am now writing (a sort of female Gil Blas not quite so loose as Faublas) gives me much more trouble. It appears that we grow humble and difficult to be pleased as our eyes open on the glare of our own vast and melancholy deficiencies. No matter, you won't, and nobody else shall, meddle with my novel. I will tell you what would make a perfect novel — you write it all but the love scenes and send them for me to draw.

The papers forced me to allude to my person and voice, since who would like the few they admire to be impressed with the false idea of their hideousness and their coarse voice? — knowing that my voice is very good and that no time can quite spoil a fine face, though it may not be a pretty one. I told you the exact truth, namely that I am forty-three, very journalière, often joliment abattu, grace à Dieu, particularly when I can't sleep, which happens four nights out of six, handsome (for those who like the Siddonian expression) occasionally when I have slept, never very ugly in the face, and as pretty as ever in person, which, by the by, does not appear under the disguise of my costume which is as loose as my morals — to use the newspaper's expression, while in fact I am a true, faithful wife leading about as innocent a life as a hermit can well do ...

You say you are six foot broad. I should from my ear (not my grammar) say "six feet"; which word is right? I know from your writing that you are thin, bilious and severe, I should say dry, not graceful; but one wants variety, I should like your shrewd wisdom for a change; harsh it might sound to a lady's ear, after the gentle, voluptuous, graceful, luxurious Argyles or Ponsonbys, but the rude scenes of age and harshness must come and is to nous autres who have been loved and doted on, the tax upon beauty. The contrast and neglect must be borne, and borne by me like a man, for Lord

Ponsonby used to say of me that my advantage over other sweet fair ones was that besides my pretty bosom and effeminate qualities, softness of temper etc., I really was "an excellent fellow" (bon camarade). So to preserve the impression in my favour, now I am growing old I must be a better fellow than ever, in which character I forgive your cut and wish you every success, every possible happiness that can be obtained in a world fait exprès pour nous enrager.

Adieu,
HARRY

One more letter follows: it is a melancholy postscript, Harriette's last appearance, written from a seedy address when she is evidently in great straits. Probably the colonel has now left her, having run through most of the money derived from the *Memoirs.* Even so, that old irrepressible note of banter still sounds. She heads her letter thus:

69 Vauxhall Bridge Road
Pimlico. Nov. 1832
Lively!
Pastoral!

I'm desperately ill, and mind wears out with body, but I fear you will be so very unhappy if you don't hear from me now and then, before I die …

She goes on to discuss Bulwer-Lytton's latest book with intelligence and spirit. She ends casually. The rest is silence.

Biographical Notes

*The Duke of Argyle whistling
and waiting for H, Wilson*

ALVANLEY, WILLIAM ARDEN, 2nd BARON, 1789–1849. At one time an officer in the Coldstream Guards. A celebrated dandy and one of the greatest wits of his day, he was described by John O'Connell (with whose son he fought a duel) as "a bloated buffoon," and by Greville as "to the last degree reckless and profligate about money; he cared not what debts he incurred." On one occasion when his debts were being compiled by a methodical friend, Alvanley discovered next day that he had overlooked one debt of £55,000. In 1831 he married Arabella, daughter of the Duke of Cleveland, but had no issue. He has been called the perfect example of a Regency buck, in both appearance and spirit.

ARGYLL, DUKE OF, GEORGE WILLIAM CAMPBELL, 6th DUKE, 1766–1839. Until his succession to the dukedom in 1806, he was the Marquis of Lorne. "An amiable, thoughtless man, who whistled away the cares of life." He possessed huge estates in Scotland, centered around Inveraray Castle. He was Vice-Admiral of the West Coast of Scotland, Keeper of the Great Seal, and later Steward of the Household to King William IV and Queen Victoria. In 181a he married Caroline Elizabeth, the former wife of the 1st Marquis of Anglesey, whom she had divorced.

BEAUFORT, DUKE OF, HENRY CHARLES SOMERSET, 6th DUKE, 1766–1835. Head of one of the noblest English families, (a descendant of John of Gaunt), and father of the Marquis of Worcester, Harriette Wilson's lover. He was Lord Lieutenant of the Counties of Monmouth, Brecknock and Gloucester, Lord High Steward of Bristol, Warden of the Forest of Dean, etc. He married Charlotte Sophia Leveson-Gower, daughter of the 1st Marquis of Stafford, and sister of Lord Granville Leveson-Gower.

BERRI, DUC DE, CHARLES FERDINAND DE BOURBON, 1778–1820. A Prince of the Blood, second son of the Comte d'Artois (later Charles X). Born at Versailles, he emigrated during the Revolution, and was with the army of Condé and arrived in England in 1801, where he rejoined his family. The Duc de Berri fought against Napoleon and entered Paris with the Allies in 1814 and 1815 where he became notorious for the license of his conduct. In 1816 he married Princess Caroline of Naples; a charming, gay, courageous girl through whom the degenerate French monarchy hoped to re-establish itself firmly. (It was said that of all of them, the Duc de Berri was the only prince capable of begetting an heir.) However, his first two children died in infancy. In 1820, some months before the birth of the Duchesse de Berri's third child, the Duke was assassinated one night as he left the opera. His posthumous child, the Comte de Chambord (Henri V), lived, for the most part, banished from France.

BERWICK, LORD, THOMAS NOEL HILL, BARON BERWICK OF ALTINGHAM, 1770–1832. He married at St. Marylebone, on 8 February, 1812, Sophia (a minor), daughter of John Dubochet. Lord Berwick died at Naples. His widow survived him by forty-three years, expiring at Leamington in 1875.

BROUGHAM, LORD, HENRY BROUGHAM, 1st VISCOUNT BROUGHAM AND VAUX, 1778–1868. The great advocate, Lord Chancellor and the defender of Queen Caroline at her trial for adultery in 1820. Brougham first emerges as a feared and hated force in politics around 1812. An ornament of Whig society, his cynical nature earned him the nicknames of "Wickedshifts" and "Beelzebub" given him by the diarist Creevey. His enthusiasm for the South of France first launched the little town of Cannes as a fashionable center.

Creevey, whose sharp eyes remarked most things, tells us that "Brougham's hatred of her (his wife), absolute hatred, is too visible." Brougham married a Mrs. Spalding, daughter of Thomas Eden. Creevey found her the ugliest of her sex, the most unaccountable person he had ever known. "A Gentleman's Daughter who resembled the commonest Pot Girl." He accused her of being "forever on the languishing tack instead of the cursing and swearing she is so distinctly made for."

BRUMMELL, GEORGE, "THE BEAU," 1778–1840. Although of comparatively humble origin his name has become the synonym for elegance. His father, the son of a valet, had risen in the world until he became Secretary to the Prime Minister, Lord North. He was later High Sheriff for Berkshire. George was sent to Eton where, handsome, clever and a good sportsman, he laid the foundations for his entry into the beau monde where he became the protégé of Georgiana, Duchess of Devonshire. He rapidly rose to a position of supremacy among the ton. He was their *arbiter elegantiarum*. Although he never appeared to be particularly interested in any one woman, all of them fought to secure his presence in their opera boxes or at their dinners. He was a cold fish, egocentric to the point of madness, a calculating arriviste who reckoned on his audacity to carry him along at a rate of living few could afford. The Prince of Wales made much of him until the Beau's arrogance became insufferable. Byron said of the fit of Brummell's coat that "it seemed as if the body thought." His follies, extravagances and love of high play at last ruined him. Swamped in debts, he fled his creditors to France where the good offices of his remaining friends eventually obtained him the post of British Consul at Caen. Soon his creditors there, too, began pressing him. An awful specter of his former self, he died insane, in conditions of abject misery, cared for at the last by the Sisters of Charity.

BYRON, LORD, GEORGE GORDON, 6th BARON BYRON, 1788–1824. The celebrated poet whose verses inflamed the public from one end of Europe to the other. A sulky, spoiled Adonis, whose genius did not excuse his boorishness. A poseur who drank vinegar to keep his figure and whose "Byronic curls" were maintained by curl-papers, according to one eyewitness. A most fascinating rebel, he was embroiled in scandals without number and at last fled England for the Near East. He dabbled in Orientalism, swam the Hellespont and settled in Italy. The infatuated Lady Caroline Lamb summed him up as "mad, bad, and dangerous to know," which must have delighted the poet since he liked nothing better than to pose as daemonic. Mme. de Staël found his prevailing mood one of profound melancholy. He was irresistible to all kinds of women, who smothered him by their advances. In spite of his envied attraction for women he was unable to enjoy his conquests, sacrificed love to vanity, and looked, said Stendhal, "like Talma in the role of Nero. He suffered from his ostracism, though he took a sort of masochistic enjoyment in fostering it, and silly women would run out of the room as he entered ... . His own caste revenged themselves on the *writer*, by persecuting the man, though they could not succeed in snubbing his birth, or breeding, or brilliance." He contracted a most disastrous marriage to Miss Milbanke, niece of Lady Melbourne, and died young, disillusioned and splenetic, fighting for Greek independence. Childe Harold's pilgrimage was done.

CARYSFORT, LORD, JOHN JOSHUA PROBY, 1st EARL, 1751–1828. Joint Postmaster General and Keeper of the Rolls in Ireland. A cultivated, poetically inclined individual, always much grieved at the conduct of his niece, Julia Storer (or Johnstone).

RAVEN, LORD, WILLIAM CRAVEN, 2nd EARL OF CRAVEN, 1770–1825. Son of Elizabeth, Lady Craven, the intrepid traveler, who married, *en secondes noces*, the Margrave of Ansbach and Brandenburg. Lord Craven was Colonel of the 84th Foot, Aide-de-Camp to the King, 1798–1805, Lord Lieutenant of Berkshire. In 1807 he married a provincial actress, Louisa Brunton, whose father, once a greengrocer in Drury Lane, had become manager of the Norwich Theater, where Louisa appeared with considerable success.

DEERHURST, LORD, GEORGE WILLIAM COVENTRY, 10th EARL OF COVENTRY, 1784–1843. An eccentric who always appeared to be in a great hurry; known for his habit of rushing down Piccadilly after any pretty passer-by. "Unusually sparing of soap and water," in 1811 he married, *en secondes noces*, "Mary with £100,000," daughter of the 6th Duke of St. Albans. He grew more and more intractable until at last he died insane.

DEVONSHIRE, DUKE OF, WILLIAM GEORGE SPENCER CAVENDISH, 6th DUKE OF DEVONSHIRE, 1790–1858. Son of the celebrated Georgiana, Duchess of Devonshire, he succeeded to the title in 1811. Enormously wealthy, he was Lord Chamberlain of the Household and Ambassador Extraordinary to St. Petersburg at the coronation of the Czar Nicholas I, a special mission which was said to have cost him £50,000 over and above the sum granted by his government. Perhaps owing to his deafness, he led a rather retired life, concentrating his energies on Joseph Paxton's designs for laying out the gardens at Chatsworth, and the erection of a conservatory which covered an acre of ground. He was to some a benign, poetic figure, to others very cold and aloof. He never married but appears to have been, in his youth, something of a social force. Raikes speaks of him as having launched the waltz on English society. "No event ever produced so great a sensation ... as the introduction of the German waltz in 1813. Up to that time the English country dances, Scotch steps, and an occasional Highland reel formed the evening recreation of the first circles. But peace was drawing near, foreigners were arriving, and the taste for Continental customs and manners became the order of the day. The young Duke of Devonshire, as the Magnus Apollo of the London drawing rooms, was at the head of these innovations ... Old and young returned to school, and the mornings which had been dedicated to lounging in the Park were now absorbed at home in practicing the figures of the French quadrille, or whirling a chair round the room to learn the step and measure of a German waltz. ... What scenes have we witnessed in those days at Almack's, etc! What fear and trembling in the debutantes at the commencement of a waltz, and what giddiness and confusion at the end! It was perhaps owing to the latter circumstance that so violent an opposition soon arose to this new recreation on the score of morality. The anti-waltzing party took the alarm, cried it down, mothers forbade it, and every ballroom became a scene of feud and contention."

EBRINGTON, LORD. HUGH FORTESCUE, 2nd EARL FORTESCUE OF CASTLE HILL, 1783–1861. Viscount Ebrington until 1841, he was M.P. for Barnstaple, 1801–7,

Viceroy of Ireland, 1839–41. Lord Steward of the Household to Queen Victoria, 1841–50. Not much is known about this gentleman. He appears to have been of a studious character, which is not, however, the impression Harriette gives. He obtained his M.A. at Oxford in 1810 and became a Fellow of the Royal Society in 1817. His widow survived him for thirty-five years, only dying, at the age of ninety-one, in 1896.

ELLICE, EDWARD ("BEAR"), OF INVERGARRY, 1781–1863. M.P. for Coventry and Secretary to the Treasury, an influential Whig politician whose fortune derived from enormous properties in Canada. He married first Lady Hannah, sister of Earl Grey; and later. Lady Leicester, widow of the 1st Earl.

FIFE, LORD, JAMES DUFF, 4th EARL OF FIFE, 1776–1857. Major General in the Spanish army and a great ladykiller. Protector of La Mercandotti, the celebrated Spanish ballerina who became the rage of London at the age of fifteen. Lord Fife was said by some to be her father. In any case he lost her to the wealthy dandy, "Golden Ball" Hughes. A current couplet read: "The fair damsel is gone, and no wonder at all That bred to the dance she has gone to the Ball."

FITZCLARENCE, CAPTAIN GEORGE, 1794–1842. One of the ten children born to the Duke of Clarence (later King William IV) and Mrs. Jordan, the actress. In 1831 he was created Earl of Munster.

FREELING, MR., LATER SIR GEORGE HENRY FREELING, 1789–1841. Commissioner of Customs and the inaugurator of various reforms in the Postal Service.

GUICHE, DUC DE, ANTOINE GENEVIÈVE HARACLIUS AGÉNOR, DUC DE GRAMONT, 1789–1855. Holder of one of the greatest titles in France, he was born at Versailles in the first year of the Revolution. His family emigrated to Russia, then to England. At the age of nine, the young Comte de Gramont (as he then was) was given the brevet rank of 2nd Lieutenant in the Russian Regiment of Tauride. Arrived in England in 1802 at the age of thirteen, he was given a commission in the Prince of Wales' regiment, the 10th Hussars, which paid for his education. He fought against Napoleon under the English colors. He was a universal favorite, dazzlingly handsome and considered perfectly irresistible to women, according to Gronow, who also stated he was "a grand seigneur in word and deed, quiet in manner, a chivalrous, high-minded man. The most perfect gentleman I ever met with in any country." He married the beautiful sister of Comte d'Orsay, the dandy, succeeded his father as Duc de Gramont in 1836 and died in Paris where he had returned with the Bourbons. It is of interest to recall that it was his son, the Comte de Gramont, born in 1819, who became the protector of Marie Duplessis, the original of the *Dame aux Camélias* and first launched her in the world of Parisian high gallantry. In 1848 he married the daughter of Lord Mackinnon and, entering the Diplomatic Service, was Ambassador to Rome during the formation of the Kingdom of Italy. In 1870 he was Minister of Foreign Affairs, a position he did not fill with distinction, for when war was declared against Prussia and the French saw that Germany was uniting against them contrary to what the Duc de Gramont had led them to believe, he was forced to resign. He lived retired, embittered, a finished man and one who is remembered less for having been Minister of Foreign Affairs than for having been the lover of *La Dame aux Camélias*.

HERTFORD, LORD, FRANCIS CHARLES SEYMOUR-
CONWAY, 3rd MARQUIS, 1777–1842. Sometimes referred to
in the *Memoirs* by his earlier title of Lord Yarmouth. A wealthy,
dissolute man of appetites, who appeared to some of his contemporaries to have no single redeeming feature but who
appears very favorably in the *Memoirs*. His mother, the second
Marchioness, was for some while mistress of the Prince Regent
and during this time Lord Yarmouth enjoyed every royal favor.
In 1812 he was appointed Vice Chamberlain of the Household.
In 1798 he married Maria Emily, putative daughter of the Duke
of Queensberry ("Old Q") by the Marchesa Fagniani. Lord
Hertford appears as the Marquis of Steyne in *Vanity Fair*, and
as the Marquis of Monmouth in *Coningsby*, Greville harshly
wrote of him, "No such example of undisguised debauchery was
ever exhibited in the world." In his late sixties, when he was
broken with various infirmities and suffering from a paralysis of
the tongue, "he was in the habit of travelling about with a
company of prostitutes who formed his principal society. What
a life, terminating in what a death! Without a serious thought or
a kindly feeling ... faculties far beyond mediocrity, wasted and
degraded, immersed in pride without dignity, in avarice and
sensuality ... all his relatives estranged from him and surrounded
to the last by a venal harem who pandered to his disgusting
exigencies." Thus Greville in a severe obituary. It is perhaps
worth extending this note to speak of Lord Hertford's two sons,
if they were such, which is open to doubt, though he accepted
the eldest as his heir and the second. Lord Henry Seymour, as
his son, though he cut him off without a penny. Both were
celebrated characters in Parisian life. The 4th Marquis was a
great collector and connoisseur of French art. He left his
fabulous possessions to his secretary. Sir Richard Wallace. Sir
Richard passed as his secretary, was said to be his son, but was

in all probability yet another illegitimate son of La Fagniani. Eventually Sir Richard bequeathed his treasures to the British nation and they are known today as the Wallace Collection, housed in Hertford House, London.

La Fagniani's other son, Lord Henry Seymour, although never acknowledged by his father, inherited a vast fortune from his mother and lived in Paris, where he passed into history as the personification of the crazy, rich English milord. In fact, he never set foot in England. He was dubbed "Milord l'Arsouille" — Milord the Oaf — and was an eccentric, cruel, caustic dandy, spendthrift and sportsman, who spent his life among jockeys and prostitutes. "Please put my boots outside the door," he is said to have commanded one of these charmers. "They will return the compliment before long." He founded the Jockey Club de France, was its first president and may be said to have established horse racing in France. Eugène Lami has left a picture, *Calèche de Lord Seymour*, during Carnival in 1835, in which we can see the wild, extravagant way of life this man personified.

LAMB, LADY CAROLINE, 1785–1828. Only daughter of the Earl of Bessborough. "The cleverest, most agreeable, absurd, amiable, perplexing, dangerous, fascinating little being that lives," said Byron, before her frenzied pursuit exasperated him. She married William Lamb, later Lord Melbourne. Their only son died young, mentally defective. Her conduct was too startling even for the tolerant Whig aristocracy to which she belonged. Her infatuation for Byron led her to dress as a page and follow him from house to house, and culminated in a scene at a ball where she slashed her wrists with a broken glass, determined that all the world should be aware of her emotions. After her husband separated from her she lived at Brocket, their Hertfordshire home. By a strange chance, out driving one day, she encountered Byron's funeral cortège. The shock of this increased her eccentricity to the point of near madness. She died of dropsy, age forty-two, still on affectionate terms with her forbearing husband, who had continued to visit her during all the years of her estrangement.

LAMB, FREDERICK JAMES, 3rd VISCOUNT MELBOURNE, 1782–1853. Third son of the 1st Lord Melbourne. A rather ponderous young man and, although considered "a sad dog with the ladies," quite eclipsed by his brother William. He was gazetted to the Royal Horse Guards in 1803, and left the army to enter the diplomatic service in 1810, becoming Minister to Madrid in 1825. In 1841 he married Alexandrina, Countess von Maltzan, daughter of the Prussian Envoy to the Court of Vienna. In 1839 he was created Baron Beauvale of Beauvale, and succeeded his brother as Lord Melbourne in 1848. His widow survived until 1894.

LAMB, WILLIAM, 2nd VISCOUNT MELBOURNE, 1779–1848. A perfect example of the cynical Whig aristocrat, although, in fact, a very moderate Whig and opposed to all the more progressive measures. "Why not leave it alone?" was a favourite phrase of his. He liked "easy men" and an easy life, but married Lady Caroline Lamb whose eccentric behavior and infatuation for Lord Byron caused convulsive scandals and brought about their separation. In 1828 Creevey wrote, "Never man was so improved as Wm. Lamb, whether from gaining his title or losing his wife I know not." He was a fine classical scholar, "exceedingly handsome, good-natured, often paradoxical, coarse, terse, epigrammatic, acute, droll, with fits of silence and abstraction." In his sixties he became the young Queen Victoria's adored Prime Minister and confidant, the supreme power behind the throne until, at last, his place was taken by the Prince Consort.

LEINSTER, DUKE OF, AUGUSTUS FREDERICK FITZGERALD, 1791–1874. This Irish duke was the godson of the Prince of Wales. Educated at Eton from 1806 to 1810, he appears to have been scarcely out of school before he was ensnared in Harriette Wilson's coils. It would seem he was handsome, parsimonious, prudent and not a very taking young man. In 1818 he married Charlotte Augusta, daughter of the Earl of Harrington, and did not figure greatly in any of the contemporary memoirs, living chiefly on his Irish estates.

LEVESON-GOWER, GEORGE, AS HE IS CALLED IN THE *MEMOIRS*, PROPERLY GRANVILLE, 1st EARL GRANVILLE, 1773–1846. Son of the 1st Marquis of Stafford. A complacent Apollo, for many years the lover of Lady Bessborough and a pampered favorite of Whig society. His mother wrote in 1794, warning him against "*artful women …* You have a naturally pleasing manner, are well-looking, and have a good understanding." Married in 1809 to Lady Bessborough's niece, Harriet, daughter of the 5th Duke of Devonshire, he was Ambassador to Paris, 1822–1841.

LUTTRELL, COLONEL, 1757–1849. A natural son of the 2nd Earl of Cadhampton. He was a brilliant wit, "the last of the conversationalists," and an inseparable friend of the poet, the funereal-looking Samuel Rogers. Luttrell was a most agreeable man whose fine intellect was concealed, like his kind heart, behind a frivolous and cynical façade.

MELBOURNE, LORD PENISTON LAMB, 1st VISCOUNT, 1744–1828. Father of Fred Lamb, Harriette's protector. The son of Sir Matthew Lamb, he was created Lord Melbourne of Kilmore in 1770. He was made Gentleman of the Bedchamber to the Prince of Wales in 1784, and became an English peer in 1815. Brocket Hall, Hertfordshire, was the family estate and, in London, Melbourne House was an important center of Whig politics. He married Elizabeth (1749-1816), daughter of Sir Ralph Milbanke of Halnaby, Yorkshire, a fascinating and astute woman whose charms considerably furthered her husband's career. Her friendship with the Prince of Wales accounted for many of Lord Melbourne's advancements. Her children were said to be by different fathers; it was commonly held that William Lamb, later 2nd Viscount Melbourne, was the son of Lord Egremont; but she and her husband always remained on the best of terms and no one disputed that she was a devoted mother. "As long as she lived she kept me right," wrote William after her death. She was Byron's adored confidante, "*ma tante*"; it was her niece, Miss Milbanke, "the Princess of Parallelograms," who became his unhappy bride.

MILDMAY, SIR HARRY, 4th BARONET, 1787–1848. M.P. for the city of Winchester; in 1809 he married Charlotte Bouverie, who died in 1810.

PALMELLA, COUNT DE SOUZA HOLSTEIN (AFTERWARDS DUKE OF PALMELLA), 1786–1850. Regent of Portugal in 1830. Portuguese Ambassador to the Court of St. James's. Ugly, swarthy and wealthy, he was very much fêted. During the Peninsular campaign, when the Portuguese soldiers were subsidized by the English army, Portugal was a key nation, and Palmella ranked with such ambassadors as Esterhazy and

Talleyrand. In 1813 Wellington told Lord Liverpool, "the Portuguese are now the fitting cocks of the army. I believe we owe their merits more to the care we have taken of their pockets and their bellies than to the (military) instructions we have given them."

PALMERSTON, LORD, HENRY JOHN TEMPLE, 3rd VISCOUNT PALMERSTON, 1784–1865. The great Foreign Secretary, Home Secretary and Prime Minister, whose distinguished career continued far into Queen Victoria's reign. In his salad days he enjoyed what Gronow described as "the mazy waltz," and was constantly at Almack's, one of the first to essay this exotic measure; he was, says Gronow, "to be seen describing an infinite number of circles with Princess de Lieven."

PETERSHAM, LORD. *See* STANHOPE, CHARLES.

PONSONBY, LORD, JOHN ERIC PONSONBY, 2nd BARON and LATER 1st VISCOUNT PONSONBY OF IMOKILLY, 1770?–1855. "The handsomest man of his time," who on one occasion owed his life to his good looks. As a young man he was in Paris during the Revolution when feeling ran very high against England and every Englishman was held to be an agent of *ce sacré Pitt*. Several were hanged from street lampposts before any arguments or protestations could begin. As the young Ponsonby was walking down rue St. Honoré, he was seized by an infuriated mob, yelling their bloodcurdling cry *à la lanterne!* as they set about stringing him up to the nearest lamp post. The noose was round his neck and he had been jerked off the ground when some of the women rushed forward, cut the cord and freed him, crying that he was too handsome a boy to hang.

Besides the powerful effect of his good looks, Ponsonby was said to possess "a tact and perfection of manner which rendered him irresistible." He succeeded his father in 1806. In 1803 he had married Lady Frances Villiers, daughter of the 4th Earl of Jersey. A portrait of her by Opie shows a grave, dark, classically beautiful young creature, the loveliest debutante of the season. Ponsonby fell in love on sight and they were married before she was sixteen. She lived rather apart from the world, being very shy and deaf—the legacy of an attack of scarlet fever. Her husband was said to be always much in love with her, but always at great pains to conceal it from her too. In 1825 Lord Ponsonby was appointed Ambassador to Buenos Aires, to Constantinople in 1832 and to Vienna in 1846. He made a most admirable ambassador, although he abhorred making speeches. Sir John Drummond-Hay, one of his staff at the Porte, recounts that when the Ambassador was received by the Sultan for the first time, in great state, he struck an attitude and, with an impassive face, majestically counted up to fifty, pausing occasionally on a number, smiling on others, raising his voice in emphasis and ending "forty-eight ... forty-nine, *fifty!*" as if it were some particularly felicitous phrase. The Turks, who could not understand a word of English, appeared much gratified. The Ambassador's interpreter then stepped forward and read in Turkish the excellent speech which the Ambassador had prepared and the ceremony finished in style with the Sultan graciously replying and Lord Ponsonby, with further bows, continuing to count impressively from fifty up to eighty. On leaving he explained to his bewildered staff that he wasn't going to be bothered to memorize a speech that none of the Sublime Porte could understand anyhow.

Another example of his highly unconventional but practical methods is recounted by Major General Sir John Ponsonby in his book on the Ponsonby family. On one occasion the Sultan, feeling that the *Corps Diplomatique,* headed by Lord Ponsonby, did not show sufficient humility and sufficient awe when entering the Royal presence, caused a very low door to be built, through which the diplomats had to pass to enter the Hall of Audience. This door was so low that it was necessary to crawl through on all fours. Lord Ponsonby, suddenly confronted with the new door, turned round without a moment's hesitation and crawled through backwards, presenting a splendid expanse of white satin breeches to the waiting Sultan and his viziers. This, said one of his attachés, was typical of Lord Ponsonby, of his coolness, his sense of humor and his practical methods of dealing with unexpected situations.

PONSONBY, (JOHN) WILLIAM 4th EARL OF BESSBOROUGH, 1781–1847. Home Secretary under Lord Melbourne, 1834–5, Lord Lieutenant of Carlow and Kilkenny, in Ireland, 1846–7. In 1805 he married a daughter of the Earl of Westmoreland. His mother was the celebrated Lady Bessborough who, with her sister Georgiana, Duchess of Devonshire, queened it over Whig society and has left us such entrancing letters. His sister was the mercurial Lady Caroline Lamb.

REGENT, THE PRINCE, AFTERWARDS GEORGE IV, 1762–1830. The First Gentleman of Europe, a great patron of the arts, who continued the Royal Collections begun by Charles I, and the first monarch since Charles II to be fashionable. He was a sportsman, dandy and débauché, and possessed great personal charm, which, however, he did not always care to exercise. His behavior towards both Mrs. Fitzherbert, his unacknowledged wife, and Queen Caroline, his consort, was odious. He was greatly under the sway of his successive mistresses, from whom he took his tone, often with deplorable results. His excesses finally destroyed his health and looks and he died, a dropsical wreck, no trace left of the dazzling figure once known as Prince Florizel.

SOMERSET, LORD CHARLES, 1767–1831. Brother of the 6th Duke of Beaufort. Governor of the Cape of Good Hope, a sermonizing sort of man who spent much time trying to prevent his nephew, Lord Worcester, from becoming involved with Harriette Wilson.

SOMERSET, THE REV. LORD WILLIAM, PREBENDARY OF BRISTOL, 1784–1851. Another of Lord Worcester's uncles also employed by the Beaufort family in their efforts to dissuade the Marquis from marrying Harriette. A celebrated whip, he loved to drive, but being too poor to afford his own curricle, he often acted as "Tiger" to his friend Lord Berwick.

STANHOPE, CHARLES, 4th EARL OF HARRINGTON, 1780–1851. Better known as Lord Petersham, which title he held until 1829. One of the most celebrated of the Regency bucks, a captain in the Prince of Wales Light Dragoons, Lord of the Bedchamber, 1812–20. The perfect example of a dandy. His dun-colored liveries were inspired by those of the French noblesse. Lady Bessborough believed he wore stays, "what Misses us'd to wear some years ago." He collected rare kinds of snuff and exotic teas, and never ventured out before six o'clock in the evening when he was to be seen strolling down St. James's, or lolling and lisping among his fellow dandies at White's. His manner was as affected as his lisp and he wore, (a great rarity at that time), a little pointed beard expressly to emphasize his alleged likeness to Henri IV.

STANHOPE, LEICESTER, LATER 5th EARL OF HARRINGTON, 1784–1862. The third son of the 3rd Earl, he succeeded his brother, Lord Petersham, in the earldom of Harrington. Colonel of the 1st Life Guards, Deputy Quartermaster General, 1817–1821. Deputy Adjutant General in the East Indies, 1815–17, where he saw considerable service. He travelled to Greece on questions of Greek independence, where he met Byron, and after the poet's death he brought home his remains. In 1831 he married Elizabeth, daughter of William Green of Jamaica.

STOCKDALE, JOSEPH, 1770–1847. Bookseller and publisher. He specialized in literature of a dubious character and was at one time concerned with various Societies for the Suppression of Vice, or organizations which called attention to such diversions as illustrated editions of Rabelais, "Generating Bedsteads", (no doubt the kind that Lady Hamilton, when still Emma Hart, had adorned and rendered so particularly lively), or those snuffboxes which contained, hidden under the lid, drawings of a most inflammatory nature and which had, we are told, "a ready Market in Boarding Schools for Young Ladies." Stockdale, who was once the young Shelley's publisher, edited Harriette's *Memoirs*. Some people think he wrote a large part of them. As Harriette's publisher he was sued for libel and damages by an insignificant person who, it is thought, was put up to taking action by a number of better known gentlemen happy to find a cat's-paw. Stockdale lost the case and had to pay heavily. Next, Mr. Fisher, the attorney and ladykiller of Devonshire who claimed Harriette had libeled him, sued Stockdale for defamation of character. Again Stockdale lost the case. He was soon ruined, being next embroiled in a series of litigations which landed him in the Debtors' Prison. During this confinement he profited by extracting from his fellow prisoners the most startling disclosures concerning a number of distinguished people. These disclosures his wife was preparing in brochure form, with a view, we suppose, to their publication or — at a price — their suppression. They do not seem to have been published, and Stockdale fades from sight — a most obnoxious character.

VORONZOV, COUNT. As we do not know his first name it is impossible to say to which one of this numerous Russian family the *Memoirs* refers. Count Simon Romanovich Voronzov (1744–1832) was Russian Ambassador to England from 1785 to 1806, when ill health obliged him to resign. However, he remained in England till his death twenty-six years later. He was brother of the celebrated Princess Dashkov who took part in the *coup d'état* which placed Catherine the Great on the throne of Russia. His son Michael became Prince Voronzov, Field Marshal and Governor of Odessa, long remembered for his unsympathetic conduct towards the poet Pushkin, then in exile in the Crimea. Count Simon's daughter married the 11th Earl of Pembroke. It is probable that the Count Voronzov mentioned in the *Memoirs* was either the young Michael, or some visiting relative. It seems unlikely that it was the Ambassador himself, though it is possible.

WARD, JOHN WILLIAM, 1st EARL AND 4th VISCOUNT DUDLEY, 1781–1833. Secretary for Foreign Affairs in Canning's administration, 1827-28. An excessively absent-minded man whose vagueness bordered on insanity and who, according to one observer, "affected to be absent but, in fact, no one ever forgot himself so seldom." He does not seem to have been an agreeable character. The Princess of Wales complained that he ate like a hog. Lady Charlotte Bury found him "an unpleasant companion at table. Then his person looks so dirty; and he has such a sneer in his laugh, and is so impious as well as grossly indecent in his conversation that I cannot like this clever man." After such opinions it is not surprising to learn that he never married.

WELLESLEY, MARQUIS OF, RICHARD COLLEY WELLESLEY, 1760–1842. Eldest son of Lord Mornington and brother of the Duke of Wellington. Governor-general of India, 1797-1805. He married Mlle. Hyacinthe Gabrielle, his mistress for nine years, by whom he had had several children prior to the marriage. He was a rigid moralist and insisted on a strict observance of the Sabbath in India among all the many different religious creeds over which he ruled so autocratically. On his return to England he appeared an embittered, "sultanized" Englishman whose direction of the Foreign Office was much criticized. He held the mob in contempt, took refuge in classical studies and the friendship of Lord Brougham. He had none of his brother Arthur's large-hearted grandeur.

WELLINGTON, DUKE OF, ARTHUR WELLESLEY, 1st DUKE, 1769–1852. Field Marshal, Ambassador, the "Iron Duke," fourth son of Garrett Wellesley, 1st Earl of Mornington, was born in Ireland about three months before Napoleon. To his mother the "Iron Duke" was just "my ugly boy Arthur" — fit food for powder; to which end he was early sent into the army. But to contemporary society, and women in particular, he was "the Beau". Very young he decided that to achieve success he must be single-minded. He burned his violin, abandoned the study of music for that of military tactics, and rose rapidly to the rank of Colonel. In 1798 his brother, Richard Colley, Marquis of Wellesley, was appointed Governor-General of India; but it was the younger brother, Arthur, then fresh from the battlefields of Seringapatam, who really ruled. On his return to Europe his brilliant series of victories in both the peninsular campaign and the Low Countries won him the nation's acclaim. Back in England, as Napoleon's conqueror he was fêted and loaded with honors. Yet, "No woman ever loved me; never in my whole life," he confided to a friend. Nevertheless, many women said they found him irresistible. He was a handsome, dashing figure, elegant and impressive, surrounded by an aura of victory. He had married an inconspicuous Irish girl, Kitty Pakenham, daughter of the Earl of Pakenham, largely, it would seem, because she had waited ten years for him. The marriage was a dismal failure. Two sons were born, but the Duke and Duchess spent little time together. The Duchess was shy, short-sighted, homely and lacking in the poise and social sense her great position demanded. The Duke remained outwardly loyal, however, and was with her when she died. His was an astute, generous, chivalrous nature, without meanness or rapacity. A great aristocrat by birth and bearing, his particular brand of common sense, tact and breadth of vision made him the confidant and arbiter of three successive sovereigns. His power was absolute over the Regent (later George IV), William IV and Queen Victoria. Indeed he was perhaps the only person to whom Queen Victoria ever deferred, once the Prince Consort had established his sway. To mark their gratitude for Wellington's final defeat of Napoleon the nation presented him with Apsley House, the somber yet splendid stone mansion which still stands at Hyde Park Corner, and which is unofficially known as No. 1, London.

WORCESTER, MARQUIS OF, HENRY SOMERSET, LATER DUKE OF BEAUFORT, 1792–1854. Dandy and sportsman; he joined the 10th Hussars in 1810 and was Aide-de-Camp to Wellington, 1812–1814, in the peninsular campaigns. Having sown his wild oats with Harriette Wilson, he settled into an unimpeachable tenor of life by marrying in 1814 the niece of the Duke of Wellington, Georgiana Frederica Fitzroy, who died in 1821. But in 1822 he married her half-sister, Emily Frances, and a contemporary letter states: "I heard by the last post of Worcester's marriage with E.F. What a complication of folly and, I should fear, eventually of misery. He never was and never can be steady to any one thing or person." He lived principally at Badminton, became M.P. for West Gloucestershire, was an admirable landlord, a great patron of field sports and Master of the Beaufort Hounds. His widow survived until 1889.

Biographical Notes on the Principal Diarists of the Regency

CREEVEY, THOMAS, 1768-1838. Diarist and letter writer, son of a Liverpool merchant and one-time sea captain, but thought very possibly the illegitimate son of Charles, 1st Earl of Sefton. He was called to the bar in 1794 and practiced between London and Liverpool. In 1802 he married the charming widow, Mrs. Ord, who, by her influence with her many high-placed friends, greatly advanced her husband's career. Creevey entered Parliament as M.P. for Thetford, nominated by the Duke of Norfolk. A warm friendship sprang up between Mrs. Creevey and Mrs. Fitzherbert, the Prince Regent's mistress or wife, and further advanced the Creeveys in those fashionable and political circles, which Creevey negotiated so adroitly.

The years passed, punctuated by delightful letters exchanged between all the members of the Creevey-Ord family, Creevey's journals, and his voluminous correspondence with friends; all these are rich sources of information on the period. Creevey missed nothing. High politics, high life, gossip, intrigue, family affairs and international politics. His pawky wit is particularly evident in the nicknames he bestowed on many of the characters of whom he writes. Lord Broughton found him not always agreeable and summed him up thus: "One who would let no principle of any kind stand in the way of his joke … He spared no one … He had that lively perception of the ridiculous which goes to make an entertaining man. Raillery of the present and destruction of the absent were his weapon for general talk; but when serious he showed sound and honest views, both of public and private duties, and discovered qualities which might adorn a higher character than he had endeavoured to acquire."

GREVILLE, CHARLES CAVENDISH FULKE, 1794–1865. Political diarist and page to George III and later private secretary to Lord Bathurst. He obtained the sinecure Reversion of the Clerkship to the Privy Council, to which he owes much of his authority in writing of the inner workings of both the political and social life of his times. His passion was horses. He was one of the oldest members of the Jockey Club and managed the racing stables of his close friend the Duke of York from 1821 to 1826. His *Memoirs* are a wonderfully evocative account of a whole age. He was an epicure, a good friend, "a loving cynic," and had that detachment and attention to detail which mark the best diarist.

GRONOW, REES-HOWELL, 1794–1865. Son of a Welsh landowner, whose estates, Court Herbert, were in Glamorgan-shire. At Eton he became the close friend of Shelley. In 1812 he was gazetted Ensign in the Guards and saw service in the Spanish campaigns. He was one of the finest dandies and men about town in the early years of the century, and one of the few officers admitted to Almack's Club, which set up to dictate to London society. The Duke of Wellington, it may be remembered, was once turned away, and went meekly, because he was not suitably dressed (said Almack's) to enter the sacred portals. Captain Gronow fought at Quatre Bras and Waterloo, and later became M.P. for Stafford. In 1831, declared bankrupt, he left London to live chiefly abroad. His *Recollections* are fascinating but often very inaccurate accounts of his life and times.

RAIKES, THOMAS, 1777–1848. Diarist. Son of the promoter of Sunday schools and, in violent contrast, close friend of the Regency dandies and often their butt — "though he did kick sometimes." A solid, sober man whose curiosity led him to record great events and small in the society of both London and Paris, the French capital being his home during the latter part of his life. His father had been a governor of the Bank of England, and his family conducted its merchant's business in the city — to the east of fashionable Mayfair. Thus to the noble snobs of St. James's and the West End where he passed his evenings, playing high at White's or Crockford's, (often with Beau Brummell, his friend since Eton), he was known as "Apollo", since he rose in the east and set in the west. His diaries range over a huge field of early nineteenth-century daily life. In 1829 he travelled to Russia. His Russian Journal gives us, besides many things of interest, a sadly unenthusiastic picture of the poet Alexander Pushkin.

About the Author

Lesley Blanch (1904-2007) influenced and inspired generations of writers, readers and critics. Her lifelong passion was for Russia, the Balkans and the Middle East. At heart a nomad, she spent the greater part of her life travelling about those remote areas her books record so vividly.

Born in London in 1904, Blanch's first career was as a book illustrator and caricaturist, and scenic and costume designer for the theatre, before turning to writing. While her reputation now rests primarily on four works of non-fiction – *The Wilder Shores of Love*, *Journey into the Mind's Eye*, *The Sabres of Paradise* and *Pierre Loti* – her early journalism brings to life the artistic melting pot that was London between the wars, and her books, something of the Middle East as it once was, before conflict and turmoil became the essence of relations between the Arab World and the West. Her only novel, *The Nine Tiger Man*, a razor-sharp romantic satire on class and Empire, is dedicated to Nancy Mitford.

She left England in 1946, never to return, except as a visitor. Her marriage to Romain Gary, the French novelist and diplomat, afforded her many years of happy wanderings. After their divorce, in 1963, Blanch was seldom at her Paris home longer than to repack.

Blanch was well ahead of her time and prescient in the way she attempted to bridge West and East – especially the West and Islam.

Blanch was modern and free, with tremendous wit and style; and a traveller who took risks and relished writing about her adventures. Her life reads like a novel and sets her apart as being a true original. She died in Menton in the South of France, age 103. Her posthumous memoirs *On the Wilder Shores of Love: A Bohemian Life* are published by Virago.

Books by Lesley Blanch

THE WILDER SHORES OF LOVE
The Stories of four ninteenth-century women who
followed the beckoning Eastern star

THE SABRES OF PARADISE
Conquest and Vengeance in the Caucasus

PIERRE LOTI
Portrait of an Escapist

PAVILIONS OF THE HEART
The Four Walls of Love

THE NINE TIGER MAN
A Satirical Romance

JOURNEY INTO THE MIND'S EYE
Fragments of an Autobiography

ON THE WILDER SHORES OF LOVE
A Bohemian Life

www.lesleyblanch.com